For Diane,

Best Regards,

Louis Rose

6/99

The South Side

The South Side

*The Racial Transformation
of an American Neighborhood*

Louis Rosen

CHICAGO   *Ivan R. Dee*   1998

Library of Congress Cataloging-in-Publication Data:
Rosen, Louis.
    The South Side : the racial transformation of an American
neighborhood / Louis Rosen.
        p.   cm.
    ISBN 1-56663-190-4 (alk. paper)
    1. Chicago (Ill.)—Race relations.   2. Afro-Americans—Illinois—
Chicago—Relations with Jews.   3. Jews—Illinois—Chicago—
Attitudes.   4. Migration, Internal—Illinois—Chicago—
History—20th century.   5. Afro-Americans—Illinois—Chicago—
Interviews.   6. Jews—Illinois—Chicago—Interviews.   I. Title.
F548.9.N4R67   1998
305.8'09773'11—dc21   98-13267

For Charlotte and Teddy

And he shall turn the heart of the fathers to the children,
and the heart of the children to their fathers,
lest I come and smite the earth with a curse.

—Malachi 4:6

The South Side

Introduction

I grew up in a white, middle-class, largely Jewish enclave on the far South Side of Chicago. The neighborhood itself had no generally accepted name, though in fact there were two names associated with it, neither one of which seemed to fit. South Shore Gardens was the official name of the section east of Jeffery Boulevard, the main north-south artery connecting our community with the rest of the city, while west of Jeffery was designated South Shore Valley. Yet most of us living in the area during the 1950s and '60s found it hard to remember which side of Jeffery was which, probably because neither name reflected the geography, landscape, or character of the neighborhood. To most of us, home was simply the South Side

The South Side is the story of this particular neighborhood— how it was built during the optimistic years that followed World

War II, how it rapidly and dramatically changed to an African-American neighborhood in the late 1960s and the profound impact this change had on families and individuals on both sides of the event. It is part memoir, drawn from my own experiences growing up in the neighborhood and witnessing the flight of whites from the perspective of one who stayed, and part oral narrative, with much of the text emerging out of many interviews I conducted with two generations of former and current residents of the community, Jewish and African-American, over a two-year period beginning in 1994.

The interviewing process began with the realization on my part that I had never spoken in depth to anyone on either side of the event about what had happened, and that the story of the flight as I had come to know it, as well as my own view of it, was undoubtedly incomplete. I soon learned that none of the individuals or couples I was meeting with had ever spoken at length about the flight with anyone either, for interviews that had been scheduled to last one or two hours often lasted three, four, or sometimes five hours as people shared their personal experiences eagerly and openly, with a penetrating emotional intensity and surprising honesty that I found extremely moving. Most seemed genuinely glad to have the opportunity to tell their individual stories, and the telling was often accompanied by the sense of discovery that can only come from revisiting an event after a significant period of time has elapsed. Even those who were initially reluctant or guarded at the beginning of our conversations usually warmed to the subject, and often offered the most heartfelt and insightful testimony.

While still in the middle of the interviewing process, and well before I knew what form the writing would take—the work was originally conceived as a theatre piece—I felt certain that the most convincing way to tell the story would be to have the voices of those interviewed do a great deal of the telling. I also knew I would concentrate my focus primarily on the Jewish and African-

American communities—African Americans for the obvious reason that they were the group that moved in, and Jews because the
Jewish community was my community; for even though all
whites in the area participated equally in the flight, I was most
personally affected by the actions of the Jewish community, and
it was toward my own community that I was most critical in the
aftermath of the event.

I further realized that I wanted to focus on individuals who
had experienced the change firsthand, for they were likely to have
been the most affected by the event. This eliminated members of
the original community who had left at the first signs of change,
and African Americans who had moved in once the transformation was essentially complete. I also sought out members from
both groups who had been involved with community affairs, hoping that some insight into the politics of the event within and between the two groups might be gained along with the more
personal points of view.

Allowing form to imitate life, I created a character on a search
who begins interviewing former and current residents of the
neighborhood where he grew up on Chicago's South Side, in an
attempt to understand the rapid racial transformation that occurred there in the late 1960s. Fourteen characters from two generations, Jewish and African-American, then join this interviewer
in telling the story, each from his or her own point of view, each
having experienced enough of the transformation that all partici-
pate in the narrative from beginning to end. These fourteen characters are drawn from the various individuals interviewed but are
composite figures, with no character meant to represent any one
person. As a result, I use fictional names and have altered biographical details (and the names of certain prominent institutions
and organizations); but the memories, thoughts, and feelings that
the characters express, and often the literal words themselves, re-
flect what was spoken during the interviews. In this way *The
South Side* crosses genres but is in spirit a work of nonfiction.

This is the tale of two groups that came together almost by accident at a particularly volatile moment in America's racial history, a tale of ordinary people struggling with the most essential issues of community, morality, justice, economics, and personal fears. *The South Side* is both a personal story and one that transcends the boundaries of specific individuals, place, and time to offer a glimpse of a struggle that is still very much a part of American life.

A Note on Neighborhood Geography
The neighborhood where I grew up, today officially named Calumet Heights, covers an expanse which can be roughly measured as slightly more than a mile at its widest points. I offer here a thumbnail geographical sketch of its borders and the areas that surround it. (Please refer to the maps on pages 16 and 17.)

The northern boundary is 87th Street, though the area immediately north to 83rd Street might be thought of as the northern outskirts of the neighborhood. The community immediately north of 83rd Street is South Shore, which had a steadily growing middle- to upper-middle-class Jewish population from the 1920s, peaking in the 1950s, at which point South Shore's African-American population was less than 1 percent.

The southern boundary is the Illinois Central Railroad tracks between 94th and 95th Streets. The neighborbood on the other side of 95th Street is Jeffery Manor, a lower-middle-class Jewish area built after World War II. Students from public grammar schools in Jeffery Manor and our neighborbood came together at the local high school.

The eastern boundary is the diagonal street South Chicago Avenue, which runs parallel with the Chicago Skyway. East of the Skyway is the older neighborhood of South Chicago, a working-class area that in the fifties and sixties had a large Mexican population along with smaller pockets of Poles, Serbians, and

Greeks. South Chicago was known as home to the steel mills and is the location of Bowen High School.

The western boundary of our neighborhood is Stony Island Boulevard. The area directly west of Stony might be thought of as the western fringe of our neighborhood. This is where the first black families who moved into the immediate area settled.

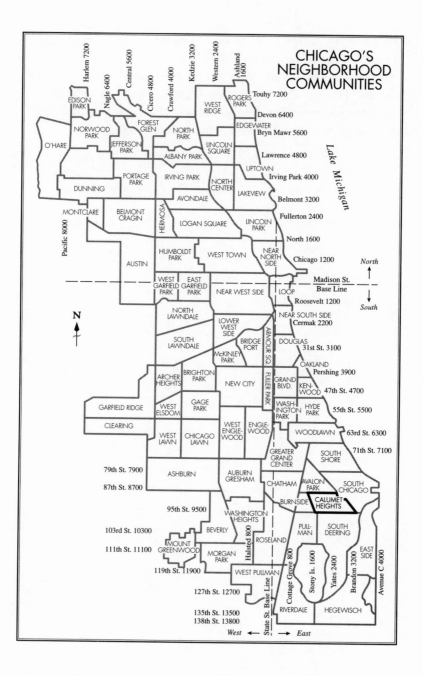

CHICAGO'S NEIGHBORHOOD COMMUNITIES

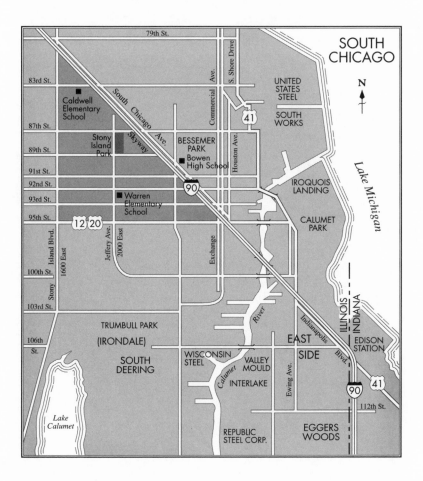

The Voices

From the Jewish Community

LAWRENCE (the interviewer). A forty-year-old former resident of this South Side neighborhood. His family moved from the neighborhood in 1975.

ARTHUR AND LOUISE DREYER. In their early seventies; one of twelve couples that founded the neighborhood synagogue. They now live in a northern suburb of Chicago.

MARILYN KIER. A widow in her late sixties. She is a former president of the board of the neighborhood Jewish Community Center and now lives in the Hyde Park area of Chicago.

JEROME AND SHIRLEY ADLER. In their mid-sixties; both were deeply involved in community affairs on the South Side, and he was an officer of the neighborhood synagogue throughout most of the 1960s. They now live in a southern suburb of Chicago.

DANIEL MAYER. Forty-four years old. Lawrence's cousin. His family moved from the neighborhood in 1975. He now lives in California.

JANE WYSOCKER. Forty-three years old; a high school friend of Lawrence and a grammar school friend of Keith Roberts and Darnell Wilson, who were among the first blacks to move into the neighborhood. She now lives in New York City.

RICHARD GOLD. Forty years old; a grammar school friend of Lawrence, he completed his last two years of high school in the northern suburbs of Chicago. He now lives in the Lincoln Park area of Chicago.

From the Black Community

KEITH ROBERTS. Forty-three years old, one of the first blacks to move into the neighborhood, and a grammar school friend of both Jane Wysocker and Darnell Wilson. He now lives in Chatham, a middle-class black neighborhood on Chicago's South Side.

DARNELL WILSON. Forty-three years old, also among the first blacks to move into the neighborhood. He was a grammar school friend of Keith Roberts and Jane Wysocker, and in 1971 worked with Lawrence in a clothing store in the neighborhood. He now owns a clothing store in the same space and lives in an integrated area of Chicago's South Side, a few miles west of where he grew up.

WILLIAM AND JEANINE GALLOWAY. In their mid-fifties. They were the second black family to move onto the block where Lawrence lived. Mr. Galloway taught at the neighborhood high school and was one of Lawrence's senior-year teachers. Both

Galloways were active in community affairs. They still live in the same house.

GERALD AND LINDA MARTIN. In their late forties. They bought their first house in the neighborhood when the massive white flight was just beginning, and their second and current home (across the street from where Lawrence used to live) four years later, when the flight was virtually complete.

Prologue

LAWRENCE

There were 205 graduates in my Warren Elementary School class of 1968; 105 were Jewish. Out of 555 students in my graduating class at Bowen High School, only 24 remained of those who had graduated with me from Warren Elementary. Eight of us were Jewish.

This happened on the South Side of Chicago, from June 1968 to June 1972.

MARILYN KIER

It was like a fire.

RICHARD GOLD

Michael Bogan was the first black kid in Warren School.

ARTHUR DREYER
There was movement coming in from Chatham from the west.

MARILYN KIER
It happened slowly at first.

JANE WYSOCKER
The first white family to leave our street was our next-door neighbor.

ARTHUR DREYER
There was movement coming from the south and north of us.

MARILYN KIER
Then once it started, it happened fast.

JANE WYSOCKER
They moved out in the middle of the night.

SHIRLEY ADLER
The first black family on our block moved three doors down from us.

ARTHUR DREYER
If you had to identify one emotion, it was fear.

JEANINE GALLOWAY
We wanted a nice place to raise our children.

LOUISE DREYER
Rabbi Fineman was standing up there preaching, "Stay. Let's keep this congregation together. I'm staying. We should all stay."

KEITH ROBERTS
We were the first black family on our block.

ARTHUR DREYER
There was fear. People talked about it.

Prologue

JANE WYSOCKER
The phone calls started.

LOUISE DREYER
The panic peddlers.

WILLIAM GALLOWAY
We were the second African-American family on the street.

JANE WYSOCKER
The realtors started blockbusting.

SHIRLEY ADLER
My friend moved out in the middle of the night.

MARILYN KIER
You have principles, and all of a sudden your principles are coming up and hitting you in the face.

ARTHUR DREYER
What you needed was one or two incidents, a robbery at knifepoint . . .

KEITH ROBERTS
You'd hear the kids start to say that they were movin'.

DARNELL WILSON
When I moved onto my block, there was one other black family.

JANE WYSOCKER
Then the street panicked.

MARILYN KIER
The floodgates had opened.

LOUISE DREYER
As soon as one moved, everybody . . .

WILLIAM GALLOWAY
We couldn't understand why people were moving out so suddenly.

JANE WYSOCKER
FOR SALE signs went up all over.

DANIEL MAYER
I remember thinking this was happening really fast.

KEITH ROBERTS
You could see the breakup of friendships.

LINDA MARTIN
They saw black people coming and they just ran.

JEROME ADLER
There was panic selling.

RICHARD GOLD
The kitchen table talk was, "Now who's moving?"

JEANINE GALLOWAY
Some were movin' out at four in the morning . . .

WILLIAM GALLOWAY
It was like having a tooth pulled for no reason.

GERALD MARTIN
Fear had been planted.

LOUISE DREYER
And the fires and the riots at the time . . .

DARNELL WILSON
Down 87th Street . . .

SHIRLEY ADLER
The rioting . . .

JANE WYSOCKER
I remember thinking, "The world has gone crazy."

KEITH ROBERTS
The kids rampaged . . .

DANIEL MAYER
Smashing windows . . .

KEITH ROBERTS
Looting . . .

DANIEL MAYER
You watched the neighborhood dissolve.

MARILYN KIER
It was rapid.

ARTHUR DREYER
It was a shock wave.

KEITH ROBERTS
Everything changed.

MARILYN KIER
It was awful.

WILLIAM GALLOWAY
It was a tidal wave.

ARTHUR DREYER
A tide.

GERALD MARTIN
We'd lived this over and over.

JEROME ADLER
It was like lava.

LINDA MARTIN
They were out.

LOUISE DREYER
It was everybody.

DARNELL WILSON
The whole nine yards.

KEITH ROBERTS
It was an exodus.

MARILYN KIER
It was an exodus.

WILLIAM GALLOWAY
We were a people reaching out.

KEITH ROBERTS
By the end, it was like a military march into a territory.
The neighborhood was finished.

LINDA MARTIN
They practically gave away some of these houses.

GERALD MARTIN
It's hard for me to even remember a lot of white people bein'
around.

.   .   .

Prologue

LAWRENCE

My old neighborhood on the South Side of Chicago looks remarkably the same today as it did thirty years ago—in fact, it looks better now. The whole area seems much greener. The fledgling trees that the city planted when I was a child are now full grown; the lawns are manicured, the evergreens are shaped and sculpted. And the houses—the small, plain, boxy, Chicago-style bungalows—have matured somehow, and grown more attractive with age.

But everyone I knew who once lived here is long gone. It was as if a neutron bomb fell on this neighborhood in the late 1960s. The buildings and the trees and the parks were left standing, but the people, the white community—my community—disappeared, and a new group of people, a black community, moved in.

This neighborhood has an extraordinary mystique for me. I see it as a lost place. To this day I know every avenue and alley by heart, but I no longer feel welcome here. It is no longer my neighborhood. When I take a drive through the area to look around, the stares that come my way from black people on the street make me feel very uncomfortable. I feel conspicuous. Walking around seems out of the question.

Yet I look at this house where I grew up, on the 8900 block of Chappel Avenue, and I think: Why couldn't my family still be living here? The house looks exactly as it did when we left it; the whole block is immaculately clean and beautiful; the area is quiet; it seems safe. And this house, this block, this neighborhood is without question the one place on the planet that I would call home.

How is it that people spent twenty years building a community, only to abandon it?

1

The 1950s: Building a Neighborhood

ARTHUR DREYER
The city put in the streets and sewers in that area sometime in the 1920s. Then the depression came and building stopped. People weren't moving around. So you had the area roughed in, ready to go—and after World War II it took off. Veterans came back and needed housing, and they were able to get VA loans, so all of these houses went up. And it wasn't an expensive area at first; most of us who lived there were just starting families.

LAWRENCE
Arthur and Louise Dreyer, now in their early seventies, are one of twelve couples that founded the neighborhood synagogue. I am unsure whether or not they will remember me—I was a class-mate of their son in elementary school—but they welcome me into their home as if I were a long-lost friend. Both are eager to talk

about our former community, Louise coming across as more emotional, Arthur more circumspect and reserved.

LOUISE DREYER
And it seemed like our block was all Jewish.

ARTHUR DREYER
Yet there was a mixture.

LOUISE DREYER
We all had little children. On summer evenings we'd sit out on our porches after the kids were in bed—we didn't have air-conditioning—and it was like one big happy family. You knew all your neighbors.

ARTHUR DREYER
I remember standing on our back porch shortly after we moved in—this would be 1951—and there wasn't a house in back of us for half a mile. It was all prairie.

LOUISE DREYER
And there were no stores yet on 87th Street.

ARTHUR DREYER
But by the time we moved to the Hill in 1958, the whole area was becoming quite built up.

LOUISE DREYER
We had the two kids by then and we needed more space. So we built our beautiful house up on the Hill. It was the last empty lot on the block, right next door to the Kiers. You know, Marilyn Kier still lives on the South Side, in Hyde Park. Have you spoken to her?

LAWRENCE
Marilyn Kier was president of the board of the neighborhood Jewish Community Center and the local PTA. Her late husband, a

*respected physician in the neighborhood, was a friend and col-
league of my father. Marilyn is an attractive and vibrant woman
in her late sixties, who seems younger than her years.*

MARILYN KIER

Ted and I were married in 1948, and a few years later we built our
house. We thought we were going to live there the rest of our
lives. You know, you start a family, you become rooted; and
everyone moved into the neighborhood at the same time. Remember, my block was called Pill Hill. That's because about four
dentists and five other physicians moved in there. (*laughs*)

It was a community comprised mainly of businessmen and
professionals. Not all the families were Jewish, but the *sense* of
the neighborhood was that it was all Jewish, because even a 50
percent Jewish neighborhood is a high-density Jewish neighborhood. So I think we felt like our world was Jewish. And once the
Jewish Community Center and the South Side Synagogue went
up, the Jewish community was definitely the strongest presence
in the neighborhood.

LOUISE DREYER

It was a dozen couples—we were the founders of the South Side
Synagogue. We had the first meeting in 1952, and the charter was
signed in '53. See, it says right here, December 3, 1953.

LAWRENCE

*Louise points to the charter, a large, framed document hanging
on their den wall. The inscription reads:*

*"5713, 5714–1952, 1953. Founders of the South Side Syna-
gogue: The names inscribed here honor persons who through
their efforts made possible the creation of this synagogue dedi-
cated to the betterment of ourselves, our children, our community
and all mankind."*

*The first twelve couples are then set apart from the many
other names with the following acknowledgment: "The above*

33

twelve families attended the first gathering to organize the congregation on December 3rd, 1952. "

ARTHUR DREYER

A curious highlight is that this was signed in a pizza restaurant over by the steel mills—after a good kosher meal, of course. (*laughs*)

LOUISE DREYER

We still have a picture of me standing over the charter and signing it.

ARTHUR DREYER

At first we had services at a couple of different churches in the neighborhood. I remember there was one where we would cover up this big cross they had—we would take the pictures of Jesus and turn them around—(*laughs*) they didn't mind.

LOUISE DREYER

We'd set up chairs, we swept the floor—

ARTHUR DREYER

And the office was at a hardware store that was owned by two of the other founders. Picture that—I mean, today a synagogue that would start up would at least go to a building and rent an office.

LOUISE DREYER

We didn't even have a post office box.

ARTHUR DREYER

And then it wasn't long before we interviewed Aaron Fineman. I was on the worship committee, and it was our responsibility to find a rabbi. Even at the first interview, we were very impressed with him, I think because of his New York orientation, his intellectual superiority; and we immediately offered him the job.

LOUISE DREYER

But Rabbi Fineman had just gotten out of the service as a chaplain, and he didn't seem too sure about what he wanted to do with his life, or where he wanted to go.

ARTHUR DREYER

So we had some temporary rabbis for about a year, and then we contacted Aaron again. This time he responded with a note that said between his compass and something else he'd find the place. (*laughs*)

LOUISE DREYER

Most New Yorkers think that once you leave Manhattan, you're camping out.

ARTHUR DREYER

When he came there were about 175 families—it was 1954—and we were growing fast.

LOUISE DREYER

At that point we began fund-raising. I think we broke ground on our first building the next year. There were already about four hundred families by then.

ARTHUR DREYER

But here's the thing I want to bring out: I remember standing outside that first small building during the first High Holiday service that we held there—and you could see a half a mile west to Stony Island Boulevard. In 1955 there still wasn't anything there yet.

LAWRENCE

Dr. Jerome Adler and his wife Shirley joined the South Side Synagogue after its founding. He was an officer of the congregation throughout the mid-1960s, and both were deeply involved in community affairs.

JEROME ADLER

I had just graduated from optometry school in 1955—and by accident I bumped into a builder who was building five hundred homes, a church, and an office building on the Southwest Side. He told me there wasn't an optometrist within two miles. So I took a lease on an office there, and that's why we settled on the South Side.

LAWRENCE

Now in his mid-sixties, Jerome is trim and rather youthful-looking. He seems to have an abundance of energy, clearly loves to talk, and speaks with a fast, animated rhythm. Shirley is the same age, slightly plump, and has a matter-of-fact attitude. I have no memory of meeting either one when I was a boy, but upon entering their home I immediately recognize Dr. Adler as one of the men who used to sit on the pulpit with the rabbi during the Sabbath morning service at the South Side Synagogue.

JEROME ADLER

And we wanted a place to worship.

SHIRLEY ADLER

You didn't want to go where my family was. He had no identity.

JEROME ADLER

I wanted to be my own person at that time. See, I grew up Orthodox while Shirley grew up in a Reform temple. So when we were first married we went to her family's shul, but it was so much like a church—I couldn't cope with that.

SHIRLEY ADLER

Then a friend of mine told us about the South Side Synagogue and Aaron Fineman.

JEROME ADLER

That there was an exciting young group of people on the Southeast Side, and, uh, hey!—so we basically moved into that area because of the synagogue. We bought a house—

SHIRLEY ADLER

In 1956.

JEROME ADLER

—And we figured, "Hey, we're gonna join this place. Let's stick our necks out and see what happens." And if you're one of those individuals who is willing to work, it doesn't take long.

SHIRLEY ADLER

I went to a sisterhood meeting at Louise Dreyer's house, and I got on a committee. Then I suggested to somebody that they involve my husband, and that was the beginning of the end. (*laughs*)

JEROME ADLER

I joined the synagogue board within a year. And then my neighbor down the block brought me to a meeting of the JCC—(*mock shouting*) "Come on Jerry, you can see how the J works too, since you love to go to meetings."

SHIRLEY ADLER

With our family living on the North Side, our neighbors became our community, and between the temple and the JCC, it was our whole life.

MARILYN KIER

Ted and I weren't very religious. The South Side Synagogue was only half a block away—very convenient—but it didn't seem fair to send our kids to a Conservative temple if we weren't going to live that way as a family. We didn't keep kosher. That's why we joined a Reform temple a few miles away in the South Shore community. But when the Jewish Community Center was built a block away from us—I think it opened in 1959—that became my world. I got involved there because I had been very active in the PTA, and someone at the J asked me to sit on the board.

It was an exciting place. At one point I think there were something like four or five hundred families that we had—families joined, and classes were included. It was modest, nothing fancy—you knew everybody—a real community center.

And the policy of the J has always been that it's open to anybody. Anybody. The only time you get threatened is if the Jewish Federation, which supplies much of the money, feels that you're serving a population that's less than half Jewish. As long as we were serving a predominantly Jewish population, they wouldn't question whether the center ought to be there.

JEROME ADLER

So, I went on the J board. And at the synagogue it didn't take long: in about five years I was running the finances, doing all the seating, fund raising. . . .

SHIRLEY ADLER

And I sat on the school board, and the Youth Commission.

JEROME ADLER

We also got really involved with the building of the big sanctuary. I was instrumental in latching on to the land. We got that land dirt cheap—$3,000. It was all rock there—nobody wanted it.

SHIRLEY ADLER

It was bad property for building.

JEROME ADLER

But the synagogue became a real powerhouse.

LOUISE DREYER

I can remember Art coming home—we had just moved into our house on the Hill, so this would have been 1958—and I wanted to put carpeting down. But he said, quote, "The congregation needs our money. We are not putting carpeting down. We are going to put our money into the building fund for the new sanctuary."

ARTHUR DREYER

Also, at that point we got a boost from two South Side synagogues that were closing not too far from us—one in Chatham and one in Englewood. By the late fifties those neighborhoods were changing—becoming black neighborhoods—and these synagogues merged with us, and with the mergers came more congregants and more money.

LOUISE DREYER

Our entire life centered on the synagogue. Friday night service was the highlight of the week.

ARTHUR DREYER

It was a place to get together, and people felt their Judaism. God, what a thrill it was the first time we walked into the new sanctuary for the High Holidays. It represented a lot of sacrifice.

LOUISE DREYER

And pride. We started it. We shoveled the dirt.

ARTHUR DREYER

And we kept growing.

SHIRLEY ADLER

The neighborhood was a very comfortable place for Jews. You could tell when there was a Jewish holiday because people would be walking to synagogue in large numbers.

LOUISE DREYER

When we'd walk out on the street for the High Holidays, we'd start to pick up people—and by the time we'd gone the two blocks to the congregation there could be twenty, thirty couples.

ARTHUR DREYER

Rabbi Fineman once suggested that we call it the Community Synagogue—everything that was going on in the community was there, the bar mitzvahs, the weddings, the parties, the services.

And we all worked—that's what knit us together. It was a beautiful group.

LOUISE DREYER

And Art always used to say that we didn't have any big givers. No one came in with $20,000. If someone gave $600 they got two permanent seats. That was a big contribution. And those seats were yours. Every week you'd sit in your seats. (*laughs*) We had a good time. We became fast friends, and you'd do everything with your friends.

JEROME ADLER
And Aaron was a terrific rabbi—

SHIRLEY ADLER
He was a wonderful speaker—

JEROME ADLER
—and really a nice guy, and everything was fine.

LOUISE DREYER
We adored him. He had a charisma.

ARTHUR DREYER
And he grew with the congregation.

LOUISE DREYER
He was also a wonderful organizer, I will say that about him. He knew every child in the school by name.

SHIRLEY ADLER
Rabbi Fineman commanded a lot of respect. You could hear a pin drop during a service. He'd stare if anybody talked—it was very intimidating. But the services were beautiful, and even though he was young, I think people really looked up to him, really respected him. He was extremely intelligent. You know, he went back to law school while he was in Chicago and became a lawyer.

JEROME ADLER

Later on he became the head of the national organization of Conservative rabbis. As a matter of fact, he influenced a number of our young men to become rabbis.

SHIRLEY ADLER

And the fact that he was young and handsome—half the girls had a crush on him. You can't imagine.

ARTHUR DREYER

At its peak the temple had almost eight hundred families, and fifteen hundred students in the Hebrew school. The school was one of the largest of its kind in the city of Chicago.

2

A Thriving Community:
The Children, 1960–1964

LAWRENCE

My parents moved into an apartment in the neighborhood in 1950, the first ones in their family to move that far south. Most of their brothers and sisters followed them into the area over the next decade and bought houses there, while my folks were still struggling to save enough money for a down payment. Then in 1961 my father's mother offered them a gift, a brother and a sister joined in with a loan, and my folks were at last able to buy our house on Chappel Avenue. It was very modest, but it was my mother's dream house. My grandmother called it a palace.

I was six years old that summer we moved in. I had lots of friends and cousins in the neighborhood to play with; Stony Island Park was at the end of my block and was my home away from home; Warren Elementary School, the JCC, and the South Side Synagogue were just up the street in the opposite direction from the park, and my Uncle Ted's built-in, backyard swimming pool—the family's summer gathering place—was only four short blocks away. These places, these people were my world.

DANIEL MAYER

By the early 1960s our neighborhood was the happening neighborhood on the South Side of Chicago. There were so many new families with kids in the area that houses were still going up on Pill Hill, and Warren Elementary had to build an annex and three lower-grade branch schools to accommodate the overcrowding. Also, by then the synagogue's big sanctuary, the JCC, and the Hebrew school had all been built, so you had this great sense of settled roots, of belonging to a big community; but there was also the feeling of excitement that comes with being part of a new neighborhood that is still evolving. In terms of when and how the area grew, I was right in the middle of it. You were at the tail end.

LAWRENCE

My older cousin Daniel and I grew up two blocks from each other, but because of the four-year difference in our ages we spent very little time together outside of family functions. Daniel speaks as if he is very sure of his thoughts, with passion and intensity.

DANIEL MAYER

It was a very tight-knit neighborhood. After school you'd spend a lot of time with your friends at someone's house, or the park, or at the JCC, which was the center of a lot of our social life. And all of your friends lived right in the community. You hardly ever had to leave.

LAWRENCE

Sports was the primary activity for most of my male friends, and the bicycle was our key mode of transportation. With a bike you

were free, you owned the neighborhood, and could travel and ex-
plore every inch of it and beyond at will.

JANE WYSOCKER

What I loved most about that neighborhood was that it was filled
with kids. I loved the fact that there were so many kids around
that you would walk to school and have a big group. My friends
and I would go home for lunch, but you'd only spend ten minutes
eating because you'd have to leave right away to be able to pick
everyone up to go back to school. There was a feeling of belonging, and you wanted to belong.

LAWRENCE

Jane Wysocker, now forty-three, was two years ahead of me when
we met and became friends in high school. The unassuming way
Jane dresses, along with a plain, short hair style, seem designed
to downplay her natural beauty. She speaks with a casual manner
that is alternately understated and animated.

JANE WYSOCKER

And we were all pretty much middle class—though there were
some slightly wealthier people. I remember one of my friends' fathers had a car phone, and we weren't exactly sure what he did—
it seemed debatable, maybe some Jewish Mafia thing. (*laughs*)

LAWRENCE

Richard Gold was one of my closest friends in the neighborhood
from the fifth grade on.

RICHARD GOLD

It was a wonderful place to grow up. My world was my friends.
My memory is of all of us spending a lot of time together—a lot
of hanging out.

LAWRENCE

Richard, at forty, strikes me as being not all that different from my
memory of his younger self, charming and bright, with an ironic
view of the world and a sharp, clear, quick style of speech.

RICHARD GOLD

As I recall, by sixth grade your house was the central meeting place for everybody—we'd all just show up there to see what was going on that day. And by then we were a little older, so we could take the Jeffery bus and go downtown to the Art Institute, or to the movies, or to buy records or wherever we wanted to go. Also, if you remember, sixth or seventh grade was when all of us from the branch schools came to Warren, so all at once there was this great merging of crowds. And that was when we were starting to hang around with girls. It was a big crowd those last few years at Warren, a huge sense of community.

DANIEL MAYER

Warren was a terrific elementary school. I think I was lucky that I grew up when I did, because in '57 or '58 Russia launched the Sputnik, and for the next few years there was this pressure that suddenly hit the public schools in America that our kids were dumber than the Russians, and that the Russians were going to intellectually and technologically kick America's ass. So I got a fabulous public education that I think people now pay $15,000 a year to get by sending their kids to private schools.

But by sixth or seventh grade I was also very aware of certain status issues at Warren, and though I never felt put down by them, they nauseated me. For instance—

JANE WYSOCKER

(*amused*) There was the way people dressed.

DANIEL MAYER

—you had to wear certain clothes to be cool.

JANE WYSOCKER

Girls wore Ladybug outfits with Villager socks and penny loafers—

RICHARD GOLD

Penny loafers—actually, they had to be Bass Weejun penny loafers. You could get the exact same pair at Sears, which is what

I had, and it was not considered the same. But the big thing was Gant shirts—

LAWRENCE

Gant shirts, with a loop on the back pleat and a certain kind of stitching across the cuff—starting around seventh grade, the snottier kids would actually sneak up behind you and try to pull your collar back to see what label was in your shirt; or try to pull the loop off the back—the ultimate test—because if the shirt was a well-made Gant, the loop was likely to come cleanly off; odds were a cheaper shirt would rip right down to the waist. I hated all of this with a passion and refused to buy into it. But I also hated the clothes from Sears, which was all my family could afford.

RICHARD GOLD

The other side of it, though, is that none of us took around-the-world vacations. I don't have a clue what car anybody drove, or how big anyone's house was; and I think that I would have been particularly sensitive to whether or not money was really a big deal there because my family didn't have much.

My strongest memory is how group-conscious a neighborhood it was. Once I got to Warren for sixth grade, the Jewish kids were the only kids I hung out with. It seemed like all of us were Jewish. That's where I felt I belonged. Everyone else was kind of exotic to me—and you didn't deal with them much, certainly not outside of school.

JANE WYSOCKER

I always had non-Jewish friends. But I went to Caldwell for elementary school—not Warren. Caldwell was at the northern edge of the neighborhood and was more diverse. The first black people that moved into the area went there—I think this was around fifth grade—and I became friends with some of them.

DANIEL MAYER

The Jewish kids in the neighborhood all went to public school, while a lot of the Gentile kids went to parochial school. Out of the thirty kids you went to class with every day, you'd see twenty-five of us at temple, at the J, or at Hebrew school. So there was always this awareness that you were Jewish, though you didn't walk around every day thinking, "I'm Jewish," or "I'm living in a Jewish neighborhood." We just were.

Still, there was always the sense of non-Jews around, some of whom were tougher—tough guys. There were physical differences between the Jewish and Gentile kids—and I'm not talking about Jewish kids not being good athletes, because a lot of them were. But if push came to shove, you knew that some of these non-Jewish kids would get into a fight and beat the shit out of somebody, and you didn't get that sense from the Jewish kids. Push came to shove, and they'd try to avoid the fight. And I was skinny—I never felt physically tough—so I'm sure that played into how conscious I was of that.

Also, a lot of the Gentile kids in our neighborhood had less money. Their fathers worked in the steel mills—a lot of them probably didn't have the expectations of going on to college. I'm not trying to make some demarcation that Jewish kids are smarter or better; it's just that the area at that time definitely had a class system. There weren't a lot of wealthy Gentiles living there. They were farther west on 95th Street, in Beverly. It was more like the poorer Gentiles lived around the Jews, (*laughs*) and the richer Gentiles didn't have to live around the Jews.

JANE WYSOCKER
The first time anyone ever made an anti-Semitic remark to me was at Caldwell. Some kid had a problem with the fact that I had made black friends, and she called me a "kike." At first I didn't even understand what she meant—I had never heard the word before.

DANIEL MAYER
And there were no black kids at Warren when I was there. It was

as if the black neighborhood started on the other side of Stony Island Boulevard—almost like you drew a chalk mark right down the middle of the street.

It was just a white neighborhood, and the real worry was the non-Jewish kids who were in gangs—we had clubs, they had gangs. The rumors were that they had knife fights and carried razors—almost West Side Storyish. For us, it was don't go too far in certain directions because you'd get your ass kicked.

RICHARD GOLD

I got the shit kicked out of me once for being a Jew. It was right on the corner of my own block. I don't remember what it was, but it was this kid—he said, "You're Jew, right?" And I said, "Yeah," and he kicked the shit out of me. But I wasn't gonna say I wasn't, even though I knew I'd get my ass kicked, and I did.

LAWRENCE

There was a fight that I witnessed one day outside Warren School that I'll never forget—this was seventh grade, spring 1967. It was between Jay Friedman, a Jewish kid who was built like a football player and had the reputation of being a fierce fighter, and Robert Ziente, who was taller but more wiry, and who, at least as far as the Jews were concerned, was a punk and a troublemaker.

Word that the fight was going to happen had buzzed through the halls that day, and a couple of hundred kids gathered after school in an empty lot a few blocks away to watch the event. Everybody there knew that whatever the provocation, this fight was tribal—the Jews against the greasers. And everyone was nervous, because there seemed to be the distinct possibility that things could get out of hand, and friends from both sides could turn the situation into an all-out brawl.

I remember that Ziente landed the first few punches and bloodied Friedman's lip; and then, in what seemed to be no time at all, Friedman literally had Ziente on his knees, with blood gushing from his nose and mouth. The coup de grace came when

49

Friedman grabbed Ziente by the hair and brutally kicked his knee into his opponent's left temple. Blood spurted all over, and Robert Ziente crumpled to the ground.

There was an audible gasp in the crowd. I remember thinking that the last blow seemed unnecessary, that the fight was already won, and that fighting now seemed stupid. We were old enough to seriously hurt each other. But I also felt the tribal pride. However ugly it was, the Jews had won the day.

RICHARD GOLD

I had a strong sense growing up that to a lot of Gentiles, you were different—you were a Jew—and that for the rest of your life, no matter what you accomplished, they would always look at you that way. I think that feeling was one of the reasons I got into the religion as deeply as I did—and I really got into it. I was at the temple almost every day. I went to Hebrew school eight hours a week, and I studied Torah and my Bar Mitzvah privately with a sweet old man, Mr. Rubivich. He was kind of a sage. I remember going into the sanctuary with him when no one else was there, taking the Torah out of the Ark—it all seemed so mysterious and magical, very powerful for me. I really loved it. And I was lucky to be chosen to work with Rubivich because most of the regular teachers in the Hebrew school weren't very good. Many of them were Israelis, and they didn't know how to get through to a bunch of kids who were more American than Jewish.

Eventually I was doing Torah readings every four or six weeks at Saturday morning services. I think at one point they started to pay us two dollars to do it, but I wasn't in it for the money. (*laughs*)

LAWRENCE

Richard and I often went together to the morning Sabbath service during those months we were preparing for our Bar Mitzvahs. He prayed with an ease and confidence that I didn't have. I could pronounce the Hebrew words flawlessly, but I would have to read the English to understand what the prayers meant. Sometimes during the Amidah, the long silent prayer, I would listen to Richard, or to the old men around me praying under their breath, chanting so quickly that it sounded like gibberish to me; and I would wonder how, at that speed, they could know what they were saying. I didn't understand then that their knowledge of the prayers, and their ability to commune with God, transcended the more primitive boundaries of language. Still, I watched them sway forward and back, and waited for the moments when they would bow so that I could imitate their rhythms.

I felt like I had no real connection to the language or the rituals. I remember standing next to Richard and wondering how he had learned them. I felt like I was on the periphery of the club that was Judaism, and that Richard was a full-fledged member.

RICHARD GOLD

I had a knack for the religion. You can't teach it. There is a natural connection that takes hold or not, and if it doesn't, you're never going to have it. Also, my mother was very religious, so I probably went to Hebrew school longer or harder than a lot of kids did.

DANIEL MAYER

It's complicated growing up Jewish. You're raised to think that Jews are the "chosen people," that we're special. But then you're also taught about the centuries of persecution that Jews have suffered going all the way back to biblical times, and at some point, maybe after you've been chased a few times by some assholes yelling, "Get the kike," or maybe once you're old enough to really understand the horror of why your friend's parents have numbers tattooed on their arms—at that point it hits home that if you're Jewish, you might someday be a target.

JANE WYSOCKER

I was never religious—my parents were second generation and very assimilated, and that's why we didn't belong to the South

51

Side Synagogue—but I always felt this strong cultural attachment to Judaism. I would talk to my grandmother about it all the time; and I remember how excited I was when she took my sister and me to see the movie *Exodus,* because Israel was a big source of pride to us, and the movie expressed that pride, especially in the years after the Holocaust. It made Jews seem strong—powerful, not just victims of persecution. That's what Israel represented. And in America, Jews fought for the underdog, for minorities and civil rights—all of this made us feel proud of being Jewish.

DANIEL MAYER

And there weren't any positive images of Jews in the media. What? You'd learn that most Jews in the public eye had changed their names so that no one would know they were Jewish! The whole Jewish thing in America is that because we're white, we can assimilate into society and not be caught. The Chinese can't do that, the blacks can't do that. Only the white Jews can do it. So there was no great sense of pride or respect outside the Jewish community about being Jewish.

That's where Rabbi Fineman was really different. He didn't fit the stereotype of a rabbi as an old man with a beard and a Yiddish accent. Rabbi Fineman was this charismatic, John F. Kennedy–type figure in the neighborhood: young, good-looking, extremely intelligent. I knew him very well. He was friends with our whole family. My dad was his dentist, I was friends with his kids.

I remember one time I was in choir practice at the temple, and Rabbi Fineman walked up to me and handed me this note for my mother, and then left. Everybody was, "Wow." They thought it was this big deal. It was as if John Kennedy had come in and handed me a personal note.

LAWRENCE

Rabbi Fineman physically reminded me of the pictures and descriptions I had seen of Abraham Lincoln—a childhood hero of

*mine—in the time before he was president. Like Lincoln, Fineman
was tall and lanky, with a gentle, almost feminine, awkward
grace. He had long arms, a full head of wavy hair, well-chiseled
prominent cheekbones, a strong jawline, lips that seemed almost
too full for the size of his mouth, and ears that were too large for
his head. But most striking of all were his eyes, variously protective, seductive, probing, welcoming, or wholly intimidating, especially to any ten-year-old boy foolish enough to talk during one of
his sermons.*

RICHARD GOLD

I was only eleven when Fineman left, but I remember that he tow-
ered over most other people—he must have been at least six-
three—and this made him seem powerful, stately.

DANIEL MAYER

He gave the greatest sermons, usually tying in current events.
And the way he gestured—he knew how to pause, and in-
flect. This wasn't just a child looking up to a guy—objectively, he
was great. Some people have a star quality. Rabbi Fineman just
had it.

RICHARD GOLD

He was an icon. I really looked up to him. For a while I considered becoming a rabbi.

DANIEL MAYER

I remember hearing rumors that he might be leaving as early as
1964, and wondering if he was going to be there for my Bar Mitzvah. That was before the black scare. But it was in the air in '64
that he might not be there forever. And selfishly, when I heard the
rumors, I was just hoping he would stay long enough to Bar Mitzvah me.

I think the whole notion that Rabbi Fineman didn't hold the
community together is a steaming pile of crap.

Prelude to Part 3

LAWRENCE

Passover—the commemoration of how the Jews were freed from bondage in Egypt—was my favorite Jewish holiday when I was a child. Slavery seemed to me an inconceivable misery, and the ten plagues struck me as a terrifying, impressive sort of justice. I think I found comfort in the thought of a protecting and avenging God.

And my favorite Jewish melody was the Passover song, "Go Down, Moses." It wasn't until I was a teenager that I discovered that this beautiful, melancholy tune wasn't a Jewish melody at all—that it was actually a black spiritual; that enslaved blacks identified with the Jewish people in the Bible and sang this song about us as a disguised way of singing about themselves and their own hopes for freedom.

When I discovered that, it made perfect sense to me, because as a child growing up during the civil rights era, I felt a sympathetic kinship with blacks. Blacks and Jews had both experienced various degrees of oppression, discrimination, and annihilation for generations, simply because of who they were. These common experiences seemed to me a bridge that connected us, and bonded us.

3

Rumblings of Change, 1964–1965

ARTHUR DREYER

It started on the other side of Stony Island Boulevard, which had always been the western border of our neighborhood. There were signs that black people were moving in there. Rabbi Fineman left at the end of 1965, so by 1964 there were signs.

There was also movement coming from the south—Jeffery Manor was showing signs of change; and South Shore just to the north of us, where I had my store, had already undergone some significant change. Then, finally, black people were starting to cross Stony Island Boulevard. So by 1965 rumors were starting to fly that change was going to take place in our neighborhood.

If you had to identify one emotion, it was fear. It came out all over—fear. People talked about it. Remember, our community was probably politically in the middle, or a little bit to the left, but a lot of the people had come out of the West Side of Chicago and tight-knit immigrant neighborhoods that were virtually 100 percent Jewish. The army was probably the first time that a lot of the men had had any real contact at all with the Gentile world—and that wouldn't have included blacks, because in World War II black troops were segregated.

So there was fear. What you needed was one or two incidents—you'd hear about a robbery at knife-point—and then the blockbusters started to move in, playing on the fear, offering to sell and in some cases buy the homes.

Then the real issue ultimately became Bowen High School. Bowen had Polish kids, Serbian kids, Catholic kids, Jewish kids—but apparently there weren't a lot of black students. And what everybody was afraid of were blacks.

So a committee formed to save Bowen High School—in fact, Rabbi Fineman was the chairman of that committee for a while before he left. Its goal was to try to redistrict the schools in the area in order to prevent the inevitable erosion of the neighborhood, the demographic change, the exodus, however you want to call it. Not a nice thing if you think about it. And obviously it didn't work. Because once black students went to Caldwell, Caldwell was part of the area for Bowen.

Ultimately, the schools did it.

LAWRENCE
Keith Roberts is a forty-three-year-old captain in the Chicago Fire Department. He has an engaging personality, is eager to tell his story, and does so in a manner both thoughtful and intense.

KEITH ROBERTS
We moved to 89th and Dante in 1964—Dante's two blocks the other side of Stony Island Boulevard from where you lived. We were the first black family on that block. It was a three-flat that my grandfather bought. My mother and I lived on the first floor, my grandmother and grandfather lived on the second floor. My

father had died when I was eight. He was killed in a robbery in the parking lot of McCormick Place after a JFK rally.

So my mother really sheltered me when we first moved in. She was like, "You are not goin' around these streets." And then someone burned a makeshift cross on our lawn that first year, and that didn't make things any more comfortable. See, the area on my side of Stony was not predominantly Jewish—it was Catholic. There was a lot of Irish. It wasn't really Jewish until you crossed the boulevard.

LAWRENCE
Keith and Jane Wysocker met at Caldwell Elementary School and have been friends ever since. He still lives on the South Side in Chatham, an area not far from our old neighborhood.

KEITH ROBERTS
When I started at Caldwell there were only sixteen blacks in the entire school. The first day there, my mother took me up and got my class schedule, and they were puttin' me into remedial classes, and my mother was pissed. She was like, "No, that's not gonna happen." Now, compared to the people who were already there, a lot of the other black kids did need these classes—but I'd been goin' to private schools up to that point. So, instead, they put me in the accelerated classes—you know, just to show her. I was the only black.

That's when I had my first run-in with somebody callin' me a nigger. Now, most of the people were very nice—that's around the time I met Jane. I was becoming friends with a lot of the kids in the class, and for someone who didn't want that to happen, callin' me a nigger was how to separate us.

But I did very well in the accelerated classes, and so what happened was that I became separated from the black kids. Although as the neighborhood changed on Dante I made friends that were black, in school all my friends were white and Jewish, because those were the kids I was in class with. I went to Bar

59

Mitzvahs; I had sleep-overs with the Jewish kids—I was assimilatin' real well. And when we all graduated Caldwell in June of '66, there were still only sixteen blacks in the graduating class.

LAWRENCE

Darnell Wilson and Keith Roberts grew up together and are the same age. Darnell is the owner of a prosperous South Side clothing store. He has an easygoing manner but chooses his words carefully.

DARNELL WILSON

My family moved in the neighborhood in September of 1964— 87th and Kenwood. Kenwood is about five blocks west of Stony Island. Keith Roberts and I lived a couple of blocks apart. When I moved on the block, there was one other black family.

Before we moved, I remember my mom said, "We movin' into a new neighborhood." She took me by the house. I said, "Okay, fine, I'll get me some new friends." Then my mom said, "You gonna have white people there." I said, "White people? What are white people?" Okay? I said, "What you mean, white people?" She say, "Where you are now is a all-black neighborhood. Where you goin' to is a mixed neighborhood." I said, "Well hey, people are people." It didn't bother me.

LAWRENCE

Darnell and I worked together at a men's store on 87th Street called Mr. D's in 1971, when he was a college freshman and I was a junior in high school.

DARNELL WILSON

So we moved into the neighborhood, and we didn't have no resistance, except . . . uh . . . there was a cross burned on our front lawn the first Halloween we were there. They were doin' that to all the black people that were movin' in. And I was like, "Wait, wait a minute, what's this," you know. But other than that, I never had nobody came right up to me and single me out because I was black.

When I first got to Caldwell Elementary, it was the sixth grade. That's when I met Keith. I think there was maybe about four or five black kids in the whole school.

It didn't bother me. The racial mix wasn't no problem. I met a lot of new friends, white and black, Jewish. I went to a couple Bar Mitzvahs. It was a real good mix. Somethin' about bein' young and bein' black is that black parents don't teach their kids about differences. So Irish, Jewish, Polish—it took me a while to think in terms of that. Personally I didn't have any problems with racialness really until I got to Bowen High School.

KEITH ROBERTS

I made friends with the black kids, but the relationships were tenuous. I was gettin' all high grades on my report card, but I couldn't show that to my black friends because they weren't gettin' those grades. It was like a big slap in the face to them. Suddenly they were like, "Whoa, look at this guy! He's a brainiac." And I felt embarrassed because now I'm different from them.

Jane was helpin' me get through that time, because I really couldn't relate to not gettin' good grades, but I just wanted to be average—regular. I did not want to be different from my people. She would say, "Well, you can't change that." I just wanted to fit in somewhere, and I knew I didn't really fit in on the Jewish side of Stony Island Boulevard.

See, the whites were, for the most part, very good, but the white guys who couldn't get my grades were jealous; so they would throw race into it. But the others would keep them in check. And I wasn't a real threat to anybody. I wasn't a jock. I wasn't takin' their girlfriends.

JANE WYSOCKER

I met Keith Roberts when we were in sixth or seventh grade. He was different from a lot of the other black kids—better educated.

I'm sure I always had a crush on him. (*laughs*) Oh, yeah, always did—and before I even understood that that was a problem. I was so naive at that point.

Keith, Darnell—these people were just my friends. Black or white wasn't that big an issue when we were younger. But a lot of times Keith was the only one in our classes—which were more of the accelerated classes—and I think in some ways Keith was more comfortable with us because he was around people as smart as he was.

KEITH ROBERTS

But because I was different from the other black kids, a lot of the white kids could separate themselves from those kids, and I had to be the bridge between the two worlds. That's where you get this chameleonlike quality, because with blacks I had to be one way—just regular—but with the white kids I could be the Keith who knew geometry or calculus, the Keith who spoke French, who played the saxophone and the drums. I could be anything you wanted me to be so I could fit in. Jane would say, "Where's the real Keith," and I'd say, "I don't even know." If you could imagine not doing your best because if you did your best, nobody liked you—that was the trap.

But Jane and I became good friends, and I was also good friends with Sheldon Katz and Miles Rybeck. Both of their families were real involved at the South Side Temple on Pill Hill, and I used to go up there with them sometimes.

ARTHUR DREYER

So, about 1965, people had started to move. And then Rabbi Fineman got a group that came to see him from a temple in another city. And he said to us, "You've got to be blind; you're like an ostrich with your head in the sand," were his very words, "if you don't see what's going on here"—that Jews were starting to move out of the neighborhood, and black people were coming in.

A lot of people said, "Rabbi, if you leave it's going to affect the shul." But we understood that he's got to live a life for his family, and do what he can to enhance his own standard.

LOUISE DREYER

But he was standing up there preaching, "Stay. Let's keep this congregation together. I'm staying. We should all stay." He preached from the pulpit constantly that we should not do it, run away—and then he went and did it.

JEROME ADLER

Aaron Fineman served with me on a lot of those committees to maintain the community, and he made a mistake in judgment—

SHIRLEY ADLER

He said he was staying in the community.

JEROME ADLER

He was young at that point—and he was an outstanding rabbi—and from the pulpit he said, "I will stay and maintain this community. Don't leave. Don't be frightened. We'll keep this temple going," and so forth.

Then, in November of '65, we went to the United Synagogue Convention in New York, and before we left we were negotiating for a new contract with Aaron. We're talking with him—just like you and I are—and we're sayin', "You gonna stay here?" And he says, "Yeah," and we said, "Well, we'll give you this and we'll give you that, and we'll pay for the house"—

SHIRLEY ADLER

But the signs were already there.

JEROME ADLER

They had already come through—

SHIRLEY ADLER

Chatham, which was just west of us.

JEROME ADLER
Chatham was gone. 71st Street, South Shore was going.

See, this was going to be an island where we could stay if the people held on. And we negotiated with the understanding that we could maintain the community with a guy like Aaron Fineman because he was strong. . . .

SHIRLEY ADLER
Strong leader. People . . .

JEROME ADLER
People respected him.

LOUISE DREYER
We adored him. But then when he saw the changes coming, he did what was best for him—which we all do in a sense. But he, rather than being the spiritual leader, acted like a businessman. He literally turned all of us off. I mean, the respect for the spiritual leader, and the respect that the children had for him—they felt very betrayed. The man changed—

ARTHUR DREYER
(*becoming uncomfortable*) You're getting into personal—

LOUISE DREYER
—from the man for whom we had the highest respect—really love. I always felt a spiritual leader was—

ARTHUR DREYER
All right, you're getting off the track.

LOUISE DREYER
—just a little bit higher—

ARTHUR DREYER
(*more intensely*) You're getting off the track.

LOUISE DREYER
No, I'm not. I'm expressing my—

ARTHUR DREYER
This has nothing to do with the community.

LOUISE DREYER
It did have.

ARTHUR DREYER
You're dealing with personalities.

LOUISE DREYER
(*passionately*) I think it did have a lot to do with the community. I think that everybody saw he was leaving and that it pushed a lot of people over.

SHIRLEY ADLER
There were big arguments within the community of the synagogue over his leaving. We actually split into a couple of factions. There was a group, like my husband—

JEROME ADLER
It caused a division—a lot of people loved him—and I guess in retrospect my feelings were different than they are now, more vocal and angry. But at that point, I felt—see, I was ascending; the president of the shul wasn't well, so I was running the temple for all practical purposes in '65, and I was really bitter about the fact that I thought Fineman pushed a lot of people out quicker by leaving. My feeling was, when the captain jumps off the ship, what do you want from the people? For the rabbi to leave, and even remotely make a statement—for example, "Well, I'm bettering myself." In a sense, that's what he said. And he was.

LOUISE DREYER
A lot of people were disillusioned by him. Then there were others

to whom the name *rabbi* is untouchable, and they couldn't admit that he did anything wrong.

ARTHUR DREYER

He had loyal friends and congregants who would never have left if he would have remained, because they loved him. But that doesn't mean he should have remained.

JEROME ADLER

With Fineman leaving, there was a group of people like myself who felt, "Damn the torpedoes, the rabbi isn't the only individual. We can survive without him. Let's just dig in our heels and hang on."

SHIRLEY ADLER

And there were those who felt he was forced out.

JEROME ADLER

(*frustrated*) Whenever you negotiate, there are negotiations. Let's face it—you had all you could do to pay your bills; you couldn't give the rabbi some exorbitant amount of money, and expenses, and a house and whatever.

SHIRLEY ADLER

So there was a group that organized at that point to support Aaron Fineman.

JEROME ADLER

Trying to get him back and give him more money.

ARTHUR DREYER

Don't forget, part of why Aaron left was all the political infighting that was going on. I remember him telling me once how Jerry Adler wanted him to do something—I don't know what it was— and Adler said to him, "You're only a paid employee here." And that really got to Aaron. He was livid.

But then there are people who blamed *me* when he left, because they said I was kind of rough on him during the negotiation, and that he left because we didn't give him what he wanted. But we gave him what he wanted, and he still left.

LOUISE DREYER

In the middle of a contract.

JEROME ADLER

So when we left for that United Synagogue Convention in November, we didn't have a signed contract—but I think we had come to a basic agreement. And then we were stunned when we got back, because all of a sudden he had a contract to go somewhere else. The feeling was, "Wow. He's leaving." That's my recollection of the thing. He wouldn't negotiate anymore.

ARTHUR DREYER

(*agitated*) I don't like the fact that all we're doing is talking about Rabbi Fineman. It sounds like this whole conversation is geared to knocking him over. It makes us feel . . . cheap.

LOUISE DREYER

I felt betrayed.

ARTHUR DREYER

So did I—at the time—but I understood.

Look, I have a fight within me as we talk about this . . . the good part of me says, "Don't say anything about him," the bad part says, "Tell it like it is," you know. . . . Lawrence, you're a member of the community, you're asking specific questions, I think that you're entitled to specific answers. You're not a stranger asking these questions.

He said to me, "I hear the call in Minneapolis, Artie, I have to answer the call." That's what he said. Aaron was a very talented person, and an ambitious person—

LOUISE DREYER

And he was out to climb up the ladder for himself—

ARTHUR DREYER

—and his family. And he did. There was a love there that I felt, and then disillusionment. Even if he had stayed, it might have taken a little longer for that neighborhood to dissolve, but it would have happened.

Look, if an attorney is with a firm, and he's got a better offer across town, he has to take the better offer. A person has to build a career. And he can't do it in a sinking situation.

LOUISE DREYER

It should have been done on the up and up. You discover they're not all they're cracked up to be. I feel had he hung in there, the community would have held a little longer.

DANIEL MAYER

(*very heated*) It's a steaming pile of crap, this notion that Rabbi Fineman didn't hold the community together. I'm sure there are people who believe that to this day.

He was a young man, and he was looking out for himself, which is okay—because he was bright, perceptive, and he was looking out on a congregation half-filled with hypocrites, and he knew it. He saw the hypocrisy in these middle- and upper-middle-class people, some of whom were at heart bigots, and he knew what was coming.

He was a young guy—if he would have stuck it out there, he might have delayed some families moving, but so what? He would have been preaching to a half-empty congregation by the end of the decade, and he knew it. People can try to say that the spiritual leader would have held it together, but that community was based on economics, it wasn't based on spirituality. I mean, it was nice that they had a synagogue, but it was about money. He saw that.

And don't forget, this was 1965. '65 was the year of the Watts riot. People were nervous. It was the first "hot summer," quote, unquote. Then there was all that talk about how the next summer was gonna be an even "hotter" summer. At the same time, blacks who could afford it were starting to make their move into more affluent neighborhoods. If you knew anything about the history of Chicago neighborhoods in 1965, you knew that if one black family moves in, everybody flees, Jewish or not, unless they can't afford to.

And the black people were just on the other side of Stony Island Boulevard at that point. *I* even understood that one day our neighborhood was going to be black no matter who was rabbi at our temple. It was the inevitable movement of this city. Black people had been segregated on the South Side for years, and now they were gonna keep moving to better neighborhoods just like everyone else was, and why not?

People might have been telling him, "We won't move if you stay—" but it wasn't gonna happen. The history of the Jewish population on the South Side of Chicago is that no community held together beyond roughly one generation's time, starting with Maxwell Street at the beginning of the century. He had to be thinking, "This ship is gonna sink. Do I jump out when it's 10 percent in the water, or do I jump out when it's 50 percent in the water?"

JEROME ADLER
(*spoken more slowly than his usual rhythm, with a quiet, almost pleading intensity*) You see, we grew with Fineman. He was a young guy. You broke bread with him. He was your *rabbi*, you understand?

SHIRLEY ADLER
He was part of your family; and he was a person. He felt your problems.

JEROME ADLER
So his leaving was very detrimental to the community. Not only to our congregants. At the same time it told the rest of the com-

munity—remember, the South Side Synagogue was the Jewish voice of the community—and his leaving sent the message that, "Hey, we ain't long for this community." That was the message I heard.

And the thing that bothered me about him leaving was not that he left—I could see that he had his own family to protect; if I was in his position, I would have probably done the same thing—it was the statements he would make from the pulpit.

DANIEL MAYER

Now, Rabbi Fineman preaching, "Stay," sounds like he was a little bit of a hypocrite. Sometimes you hope that your leaders will act on a higher moral level than the average person; but the fact of the matter is that he read the neighborhood correctly. Maybe he did not make a spiritual choice, but he assessed the situation and got his ass out before the temple caught fire!

Think about it—in 1966 he wasn't even forty years old. He was a young man with young children. He's looking out there thinking, "If I'm here five years from now, I'm not gonna have a job." And don't forget, this guy was good enough in his field to later become the leader of fifteen hundred Conservative rabbis around America. I think if you take the "blacks are coming" issue out of the picture, this was a guy who in order to realize his potential was probably gonna leave anyway.

MARILYN KIER

When Fineman left—that was upsetting. I mean, even though I wasn't a member of that congregation, I felt emotional about it: "Now the rabbi's leaving. What's next?" It was Fineman's temple. He'd been there since it went up. From my perspective on the JCC board, I read his leaving as a signal to the community that maybe it was okay to go, that the community didn't have a future.

LAWRENCE

I was eleven years old when Rabbi Fineman left. His leaving seemed incomprehensible to me. He was a towering presence; my family loved and respected him—it had never occurred to me at that young age that he would not always be there. I remember feeling deeply disappointed—cheated, that he wouldn't be the one to Bar Mitzvah me.

My sense of time in that neighborhood definitely divides the years into the period when Rabbi Fineman was there, and then everything else after. His leaving was the first, clear dividing line.

Interlude

LAWRENCE

Aaron Fineman has been the rabbi of one of the largest Conserv-
ative Jewish congregations in the United States since the early
1980s. I feel slightly nervous as I approach his synagogue office
for our appointment, aware that some part of my going to see him
has to do with the son confronting the father.

The rabbi, now in his mid-sixties, looks exactly as I remember
him and still somewhat youthful despite the white hair and the
deep lines under his eyes. His wardrobe is plain—an ordinary
suit and tie, well worn but not the least bit shabby. He greets me
with a strong handshake and kind words and questions about my
family.

We at first speak about the early days of the South Side Syna-
gogue, a time in his life that he recalls with great fondness. The
subject eventually moves to the racial tensions on the South Side

of Chicago in the early and mid-1960s, and finally, with what I at least feel to be a slight awkwardness on both of our parts, to the circumstances that led to his departure.

RABBI AARON FINEMAN

My leaving was a combination of things, with the main issue turning out to be an economic issue.

First of all, a rabbi has a very peculiar relationship with his congregation. For eleven months of the year you are the father figure, the spiritual leader; then for one month of the year it's a labor/management situation. It's their temple—you're the employee and you have to come to an agreement. At that time I wasn't making a heck of a lot, I had three small children, my family and I were living in a very small house and we needed a larger house. So I asked the congregation to purchase one up near the temple on Pill Hill—I was prepared to stay in the community— but the congregation didn't help me solve the house problem, and that created a sense of frustration.

At that point I began to look around—this was the summer of '65—and a congregation in San Francisco opened up. The city was beautiful, the dollars they offered me were far more than I was making in Chicago, and they were willing to take care of the housing problem.

Another factor was that a lot of political infighting had been going on at the South Side Synagogue over the previous year. That inevitably happens in a synagogue when the rabbi's been there a while. In this case there were some who felt, "The congregation has no business buying the rabbi a house." Others felt, "We should do what we can," because after all, churches have what they call parsonages. So that became an issue, and once a rabbi becomes the focal point of a controversy, what ultimately gets thrown into the kitty are a lot of little resentments and disappointments that people have been storing up. Those are the little pinpricks out there that begin to fester. A lot of that started; and

when you have to use up a lot of psychic energy to fight these political kinds of wars, it gets to be a drain on you.

The issue of the neighborhood changing didn't influence me
that much—I mean, I was aware of it—but there was also the
possibility that the neighborhood might have held, though I didn't
think there was a good chance of that. By 1965, early 1966—by
the time I left—the floodgates had opened. What you had was
like a slow moving wave. You could see it coming. And historically in this situation, most Jews don't stay. They just leave. So I
didn't think my staying or leaving would have an effect on the
outcome one way or the other, not even in terms of slowing down
or speeding up the process. I just thought the forces there were
beyond the control of any one person. You'd like to feel you can
control events in this field—yet you learn that you can't. In that
sense there was a feeling of futility. But in the end I had my own
issue that was cooking, and the racial issue didn't affect it—it was
the internal situation. And when I finally did leave, a lot of people
became very angry at us.

People came up to me saying this was a community under
stress now, that I should stay and help the congregation fight the
problem. I received a few letters—one in particular, where a girl
accused me of bailing out of the synagogue and the community.
And this was an issue I wrestled with. I was fully aware of the im-
plications of leaving at that particular time. But as I said, in my
own mind—and this could all be rationalization—I would have
been willing to stay. Had I been a little bit more experienced—I
was thirty-six, thirty-seven at the time—had I had a little more
skill and ability to process, to finesse the political situation better,
I might have stayed. But it got all screwed up. Looking back, *I*
could have handled it better—*they* could have handled it better.
But of course I left feeling misunderstood. That's part of the para-
noia you get in this position, because the reality is, it isn't so
much what you say to people, it's what they hear, and people are
going to hear what they want, and exactly what you don't want.

So my wife and I came to the conclusion that leaving was the best thing. And it was a hard decision. We'd been twelve years at the South Side Synagogue and two years earlier in the neighborhood. We had a lot of friends. We felt rooted there.

But we looked at all the opportunities involved in making a change, and it was exciting. I stayed through the High Holidays and then gave my resignation. I think it was January of 1966 when we left.

4

Firsts, 1966–1967

DANIEL MAYER

The first people who moved out of the neighborhood were the richest, because they could afford to. This was in '65, even before Rabbi Fineman left. The rich bastards on Pill Hill were moving to the far suburbs so they could have acreage and a big house. It was as much about affluence as anything else. That's the history of the world—that isn't Jewish. They'd been there for fifteen years, they'd done well for themselves, and those people were gonna go. But other Jews aren't buying into the neighborhood at that point because they're nervous that it's gonna change to black, and the richer Gentiles don't even want to live around the Jews. So the only other group that wanted to move up—and that neighborhood was a move up—were the middle-class or even wealthier blacks. And some of the black people they sold out to were much richer than people like us.

LAWRENCE

My friends and I used to play softball in a church parking lot that was right next door to a popular neighborhood delicatessen, and one afternoon Ernie Banks, Mr. Cub, came there to eat lunch. This was very exciting for us, because Ernie Banks was the greatest player who had ever played for the Chicago Cubs, and here he was living on Pill Hill and eating at the local deli, but this was the first time any of us had even caught a glimpse of him. Somehow my friends and I persuaded Ernie to agree to play a few innings with us when he was done eating; and an hour later, as promised, he walked out of the deli and over to our makeshift field, picked up the bat and said those three words that only Ernie Banks would say: "Let's play two."

The only thing that ever topped that was when another one of our new neighbors, Muhammad Ali, let us tag along behind him while he did his roadwork around Stony Island Park.

KEITH ROBERTS

Sheldon Katz was the first one that I remember moving. He left right after we graduated from Caldwell—that would be the summer of '66. I was surprised because his family was so active with that synagogue on Pill Hill. He was real upset about goin'. But I saw that being more about affluence. And it wasn't like everybody was leavin' at that point.

DARNELL WILSON

I just assumed that all of the people I graduated Caldwell with would go to Bowen High School. It never occurred to me they wouldn't. Then, that summer before freshman year, there seemed to be a few white kids who was leavin', but I wasn't thinkin' that this was a neighborhood that was gonna turn.

JANE WYSOCKER

The first white family to leave our street was our next-door neighbor. This was the summer of 1966, the summer before I entered high school. They literally moved out in the middle of the night. A black family moved in, and they were wonderful people. But that's when the first FOR SALE signs went up.

LAWRENCE

The first white family to sell its home to blacks on our street was our next-door neighbor. He was a crotchety old man who seemed to get a great deal of satisfaction out of cursing at me whenever I had to retrieve a wayward baseball or football from his immaculately maintained lawn. I was delighted to see him go.

RICHARD GOLD

Michael Bogan. Michael Bogan, to my recollection, was the first black kid in Warren School. It was seventh grade—this would be 1966—and he was in our home room. It was a nonevent for me on the one hand—he was just another kid and I liked him. But I think the neighborhood didn't receive him well.

I remember that asshole science teacher we had, Mr. Frech, was on Bogan's shit all the time—said things that even at that age I thought were inappropriate. There was something about how he pontificated about Bogan not being a good representative of his race or something. Whatever it was, I thought, "Shit, this kid should not have to sit through this," and I remember being deeply ashamed. That's the first time in my life I had any consciousness of race as being a factor in anything.

LAWRENCE

I remember seeing Michael Bogan coming into my class at Warren as an opportunity to demonstrate how well I had learned what I'd been taught about treating everyone the same, regardless of color; and I made a conscious effort to make him feel welcome in class and included in our activities. One recess in the middle of the school year, I invited Mike to join in the softball game my friends and I were playing, and I was bewildered and miffed when he responded with an angry, "Leave me alone." I could see the hurt in his eyes, and I simply didn't understand what I had done. It was years before I realized that my efforts to include him probably only succeeded in making him feel uncomfortable and even more aware of how he was different from the rest of us.

SHIRLEY ADLER

The first black family moved three doors from us. My girlfriend brought over brownies—but they wouldn't even talk to us. There was a fear, I think, on their part. Our little girls played together, but the adults just kept the shades drawn.

MARILYN KIER

The first black family moved onto my block right across the street from me. On the day they were moving in, I made a pot of coffee and went over to introduce myself, and I could actually see the fear on this young woman's face as she opened the door. I have never forgotten that. It made me realize how frightening it must be to face a white group. But we became friends. They were a young couple—lovely, educated, charming people. These were not people from the ghetto. These were people who could afford the housing.

JANE WYSOCKER

Then later that same summer before high school, a few of my close girlfriends from Caldwell left—it was as if their parents had just waited for them to graduate so they could move.

KEITH ROBERTS

Then when I got to Bowen—Jane was talkin' about people I only knew casually and that they were movin'. Jane knew about it more, and we started to have conversations like, "Why does it have to occur?"

And then dealin' with Bowen itself, especially for blacks—that was a whole other experience.

LAWRENCE

William Galloway was my senior-year Spanish teacher at Bowen High School and my neighbor on Chappel for seven years. He is now fifty-five years old, with hair half grey and a physique more portly than it once was. Bill's manner is thoughtful and soft-spoken in a way that gives weight to what he has to say.

WILLIAM GALLOWAY

I arrived to teach at Bowen in the fall of '67, about six months before my wife Jeanine and I moved into the neighborhood, and that gave me a taste of what the area was like.

There weren't too many black teachers at the school at that time. I remember sitting through a faculty meeting where the principal, Marie O'Brien, apologized to the white faculty for having had to hire black teachers. And there was a certain group of teachers that would hang out in the faculty lounge, and it was the sort of thing where all of a sudden the conversations they were having would completely stop when I walked into the room, or they'd make condescending remarks while pretending to be friendly—so I just stayed away from there. But I always had an ally in the assistant principal, Eli Goldberg. And after two years I was made chairman of the Language Department.

I seemed to arrive at the tail end of what had been a kind of special time at Bowen. At the point I left, in '74, the teachers who'd been there a while were calling that period from the mid-fifties through the sixties the Golden Era. Even in my first couple of years there scholarship was high, and the parents really backed up the school.

DANIEL MAYER

When I started at Bowen in '65, it was considered one of the top public high schools in the city. There was a tracking system there ranging from exceptional to remedial, and the highest levels, the honors classes, were challenging. Most of my classmates were

81

the kids I'd gone to Warren with, and a lot of us belonged to a Jewish youth organization called AZA.

I remember being conscious of the fact that the few black kids who were in honors classes with us were upper middle class— they dressed like us, they spoke like us, they were assimilated into the white culture—these kids were more whitelike. And we were friends in school, but we didn't socialize. The only time I mixed with the non-honor-class population was in the lunchroom or in gym class—and gym class was the real melting pot. That was the first time I was ever exposed to that South Chicago street-black stuff. But generally, if you didn't bother them, they didn't bother you.

JANE WYSOCKER

By the time I entered Bowen in '66, it was really a melting pot; so, it seemed that no matter who you were, there was someone there who hated you. (*laughs*) The Serbs hated the Poles, and everybody hated the Jews, and the poor blacks hated the middle-class blacks, and the Hispanic kids were fighting it out among themselves and then eventually with the black kids. It just seemed like everybody hated somebody.

KEITH ROBERTS

My freshman year there were maybe fifty blacks in my class, and thirty of us were the more middle-class kids. And we knew as soon as we walked into the place that the blacks from South Chicago didn't like us—no way. They thought we were white.

These were the mill kids. I think out of the 3,500 kids in the school at that time, no more than 10 percent were black; and a majority were these mill kids—and when they turned sixteen they would drop out to go work in the mills. We never got along with them. They'd wait to jump us at the bus stop because we were different. The only real threat I ever felt at Bowen was from these kids. We weren't fightin' with white kids—though it's not like the blacks ever had a lot of Polish or Serbian friends. In fact, except for some of the Jewish kids, the handful of us middle-class blacks—*we* didn't fit in with *anybody*.

Also, in a lot of ways, the Bowen administration tried to tell the black parents that we can't accept you at Bowen. Through counseling sessions they tried to get us Caldwell blacks to go to CVS—the vocational school on 87th Street right across from Stony Island Park. They were tryin' to get us to go there and get a trade.

DARNELL WILSON

The principal was Dr. O'Brien. I recall that she sit in her office once and told me and my mother that they never had no problems at Bowen until "you people" came. And my mother said, "Whatta you mean, you people?" And O'Brien said, "We had black kids from South Chicago, and their first or second year they drop out, or go join the steel mills or somethin', and we had very little interaction. But your kids are comin' over here, and they want to compete academically, and do the same things that the rest of the student body is doin', and this is where the problem lies." So my mother told her, "Well, I don't know what you mean by 'you people,' number one, but my son is here and I'm available, his dad is available; and you're right, he will compete academically, anytime, any type of academics you have."

So that's where it started. See, Dr. O'Brien was Irish, and the Irish people had a problem with minorities; so this administration did not want to give the black or Hispanic student bodies their fair shake. It was always, "No, you can't do this." "Can I have a pass to go to see—" "No, you can't do that . . ." There was one teacher—I can't remember his name—he called some of his students "petrified mud."

It was crazy. I went to Caldwell and I was in the same classes that the Jewish kids was, but at Bowen I felt like, "I got the same grades he had, so why is he over there and I got to be over here?"

83

KEITH ROBERTS

I was in the honors classes, and I was the only black in my class most of the time, just like it was at Caldwell. And again, I was dealin' with gettin' straight A's and feelin' like it wasn't a good character trait among my black friends. It was always, "How'd you do, Keith?" "I did okay." "Let me see your course book." "No, I left it at home."

DARNELL WILSON

I remember my sophomore year my parents had to come to school because I received my course book and they say I failed everything. And when my mother questioned them, we found out they were not gradin' me on the same level that they was gradin' the other students.

Then later in my junior year my own counselor suggested that I forget about college; that instead I should talk to a U.S. Steel representative about gettin' a job in the steel mill. So I went and took that home and, believe me, that didn't go over too well.

WILLIAM GALLOWAY

I had arguments with the administration because they were doing things like separating students in Spanish classes by race; undercover police were posing as teachers; O'Brien had spies reporting back to her about the activities of certain faculty members. They were just pitting groups and individuals against each other.

DARNELL WILSON

So the problem for us at Bowen was never the student body. If you looked at the black kids from my area, we was just like the Jewish kids we'd gone to grammar school with. We were all middle class. There was never no fistfights between blacks and whites, or Jewish and black, or even Irish and black. Our problem was the administration. And it was these things that led to the black power movement startin' at Bowen High School.

JANE WYSOCKER

My freshman year, I was friends with Keith and some of the black kids that I'd gone to grammar school with, but then we all went through that period when everybody became a bit estranged, because they were all going through the black power–separatist thing. We stayed friends in school but didn't see each other outside of it much. The sense of common ground was gone for a while.

DARNELL WILSON

I was the first president of the Afro Club at Bowen. See, when we got to Bowen, the black students were supposed to get in with some of the other programs—the chess club, the language club—but like I said, you was discouraged about gettin' to those programs. So you got an administration that is antiblack, and you got a small minority group like us dropped in a all-white, primarily Jewish environment—and with all the black power stuff goin' on at that time, naturally you gonna have a little resistance. It was like, "Look, we can't all flunk out here. We gotta get together."

KEITH ROBERTS

The black power movement was more of a fringe thing at Bowen, because there weren't that many blacks at the school; and also, whites and blacks liked each other there.

But the blacks didn't know anything about black history—it was never taught to us in school—so we wanted to learn, which was why the Afro-American History Club wanted to get some classes. We weren't bein' militant—it was just our way of sayin', "Wait a minute, we need to know."

This all got started at Bowen after the riots on the West Side of Chicago in the summer of '67. These riots were caused by a fireman who, coincidentally, I just relieved as captain in the Fire Department. He was drunk, and as he came out of the firehouse on the West Side, the truck got away from him and killed a little girl. That's what started the riots. That's also what caused the de-segregation of the Fire Department in Chicago. At that time black firemen were segregated in two firehouses—all-black firehouses. The riots caused Mayor Daley to move some of these firemen to the West Side so the black residents could see black firemen in the neighborhood, with the hope that maybe then the people wouldn't start up again throwin' rocks and burnin' the firehouses.

Boy, that was a time. Even though it wasn't happenin' in our neighborhood, you could feel the tension from it. My mother wouldn't even let me go out for a couple of days. But it was that fall after the riots when the Afro Club formed, the beginning of my sophomore year.

MARILYN KIER

After the West Side went up in flames, it seemed like even more people were talking about leaving. It was like the floodgates had opened. And a group of us at the J did not want this neighborhood to—we wanted to stabilize the neighborhood. After all, you have principles, and all of a sudden your principles are coming up and hitting you in the face. Either you live by them or you don't.

So some of us who really cared got a community council to-gether, and we asked the synagogues to join up. And then the JCC and the Jewish Council on Urban Affairs decided that we would hire a community worker in order to stabilize the neighborhood. Now, how she was going to do this we weren't really sure. But we hired this woman who worked out of the J, Jeanette D'Arcy—she was a lovely Irish redhead in her mid-twenties whose legs my brother-in-law admired a lot—(*laughs*) and we worked as an or-ganization to convince people to stay.

Jeanette went around to companies trying to encourage them to have people who were going to work for their company move into our neighborhood. That, of course, didn't work. Then the woman's auxiliary at the J started calling the neighbors, saying, you know, "Stay. The black people moving in can afford the housing. It can be an integrated area. Where else are you going to get a house like this for the money"—that sort of thing. You got lots of reassurances on the phone, but it was a losing bit. These people who lived there, their economic status had grown—a lot of them could afford a different life-style—and they were going to go. I think the mind-set became, "The South Side's going to be a black community—I want out."

But around the same time those of us on the JCC board—this was '66, '67—went downtown to persuade the Jewish Federation to let the J build a swimming pool. The beaches on the South Side were very polluted, and mainly black by then, and people were getting uncomfortable going to them; so the swimming pool was going to stabilize the neighborhood. (*laughing*)

LOUISE DREYER

After Rabbi Fineman left we were trying to hold the community together—we still had over seven hundred families in the congregation. So the synagogue board interviewed for a new rabbi, and they ended up hiring somebody because they were impressed with his voice. Rabbi Schechter. He had a voice like it came out of the heavens, but if you were really listening, he wasn't saying a damned thing. So when it was all over, what was there? Well, they found out . . . and then we were stuck with this bargain.

JEROME ADLER

Schechter came in the spring of 1966. I was running things around then. Schechter was an outstanding orator—a tremendously learned individual—and he was a goniff who beat his wife.

SHIRLEY ADLER

That's true.

JEROME ADLER

He was charismatic. He could walk into a room of forty-six people and remember everyone's name. If you could have locked him up on Saturday at sundown, and then let him out the next Friday evening for Shabbos services, he would have been okay.

He was a guy—we bought a parsonage, a house for him to live in. Okay?

ARTHUR DREYER

We made the mistake of buying him a house on Pill Hill.

JEROME ADLER

He went to Polk Brothers, bought a whole houseful of furniture— charged it to the congregation. Okay? To pay us back, a dribble at a time. Okay. Went to the bank—got a loan on the furniture. (*laughs*)

Then his wife comes to one of our board members—she's got bruises all over—says, "He's beatin' on me. I don't want to cause a stir in the congregation, but maybe you could talk to him." So we did. "Rabbi, this is bad." "I know, I know, but it's not what it seems." And a lot of people believed him and not her. Then he would approach members, charm them, "Can you lend me $1,500? Can you lend me $1,000?" And they would.

LOUISE DREYER

At the synagogue he was at before, they had to change the locks.

JEROME ADLER

We finally got him because we caught him cashing checks from the discretionary fund and taking the money.

All this deepened the chasm in the place, because there were some people who loved him—they didn't care what he did. They got mad at us for getting *rid* of him. They felt, "There's nothing wrong with him. So he's a little crooked; so he steals a little bit; so he beats his wife a little bit; so he sleeps with somebody he's not supposed to sleep with—so what? He's a wonderful speaker." You know?

SHIRLEY ADLER

But it's like a small town. We let the word out.

JEROME ADLER

Schechter lasted a year. But we couldn't just fire him. We had to set up a tribunal—a Bet Din—to get rid of him. The Rabbinical Assembly indicated to us that you just can't fire him without cause, or we'll never send you another rabbi.

And this was awful. There was even a well-respected rabbi from another South Side synagogue who had been bilked by Schechter, but when we asked him to testify he wouldn't—like he wouldn't go against one of his own. There seemed to be a kind of circling-the-wagons mentality. The whole situation was terrible. I was really traumatized.

LOUISE DREYER

We ended up having to pay out that scoundrel's contract.

ARTHUR DREYER

And then we had to get him out of that house we bought.

JEROME ADLER

But we found another rabbi who was a nice man. Bernie Steinman.

SHIRLEY ADLER

He was a nice man—not an outstanding rabbi.

JEROME ADLER

Bernie arrived for the High Holidays of 1967.

SHIRLEY ADLER

At that point, Jerry, the neighborhood was still solid.

JEROME ADLER

There were still 750 families. The synagogue was full up to the hilt with people. I'll never forget that. It blew my mind—speaking to 1,500 people.

But Bernie was bland—he was not a forceful person—and pretty soon that was a problem because people started to panic.

JANE WYSOCKER

At the time I entered Bowen in '66, with some black families already crossing Stony Island Boulevard and buying houses around where I lived, the neighborhood was obviously changing, but the change was slow—almost one block at a time. But in the fall of '67, the beginning of my sophomore year, I took a job on 87th Street at a Jewish bakery, and not a week went by without some customer saying, "We're moving to Skokie," or "I just bought a house in Flossmoor." It was as if moving to the suburbs was suddenly the new thing. And I'd hear the owner talking all the time about how her loyal customer base was eroding, and how if that kept up she would have to go out of business. Also, the customers were already starting in with, "When are you gonna move this place?" or, "Why don't you open a store up north, we're all gonna be there," and that sort of talk.

Things seemed to be changing much faster than I had anticipated, and it made me furious. As far as I was concerned, the situation forced you to take sides—you were either staying or leaving. People couldn't hide their prejudice anymore. I felt anyone who was leaving was stupid and small-minded. But if I told any of these people that my family was staying, they acted like I was crazy.

So the first hint of people leaving was in '65 and '66—those were the people who probably had more money—and by the end of '67 the middle-class move had definitely begun. The change was coming from the other side of Stony, where Keith and Darnell lived. Keith used to say that after the riots in the spring of '68, it was almost like a military march into a territory.

LAWRENCE

I was Bar Mitzvahed on a beautiful spring day in 1968. I recall it as one of the happiest days of my life. It's not that I felt a strong connection to the religious or spiritual aspects of the event; but I felt honored to stand there before a congregation as my cousins and brother and uncles and father and grandfathers had done before me, and offer myself to the ritual. It was a cultural rite of passage that I was proud to take part in.

And what I liked best was that it was a great gathering of all the people I loved, and that the celebrating lasted well into the evening with an informal get-together back at our house on Chappel.

The date was March 30, 1968. "Lady Madonna" was the current Beatles hit on the radio; the next evening LBJ announced that he would not seek reelection for the office of President of the United States; and five days later, on April 4, Martin Luther King was killed on a motel balcony in Memphis.

Interlude

ARTHUR DREYER

Chicago was a terribly polarized city in the mid- to late 1960s. It still is, but this was a time when blacks, by and large, were just beginning to develop a strong middle class. Many South Side areas that had once been white areas were now black, and some of them were teeming slums. Whites generally just stayed out of black neighborhoods, but many Jews owned stores in those areas; and it was known that some of their business practices were viewed by blacks as horrendous, while the view of some of these merchants was that there was so much pilfering and cheating that this was the only way they could come out even.

Now, the blacks moving into our area were middle class, but for the people who started to leave, I think the sense was, "The blacks are coming in. Crime will go up, the schools will go down." At its absolute worst it was, "Blacks are dirty, blacks are dumb, blacks are dope dealers. . . ." I mean, this wasn't the view of the majority, but it was there.

The issue of the text, Malachi: "Have we not all one father? hath not one God created us? why do we deal treacherously every man against his brother . . ."—you can't really teach Judaism without teaching that text, without speaking of being fair to people, pursuing justice; and this is the message that comes through on one level. But to the store owner who's been broken into or held up a few times too often—to these people who have an anger toward blacks, whatever the reason, they hear this but they don't hear it. A lot of people just ultimately said, "All this is well and good, and we mean them no harm, but we're leaving."

You ask me, "Was there racism in the Jewish community?" Sure there was racism in the Jewish community. But it was well known that a black who walked around the steel mills or the Back-of-the-Yards area at night did so at his own peril. With Jews there is no violence—that was the saving grace. When blacks started to move in, the community did not resort to violence, and that is no small thing.

5

Change, 1968

LAWRENCE

I made many trips to the South Side of Chicago in the course of interviewing current residents; and at some point I realized that I drive more conservatively there than I do on the predominantly white North Side of the city. Once I pass Hyde Park going south on Lake Shore Drive, I become cautious. I don't push the speed limit; I don't jockey back and forth between lanes; I avoid doing anything that might risk the type of confrontation that could result from cutting off another driver or getting into an accident. On the South Side of Chicago I am very aware that I am in some ways an interloper, a trespasser, a white traveler in a black neighborhood.

William Galloway, my former Spanish teacher, and his wife Jeanine, live in a house at the corner of my old block, directly across the street from Stony Island Park. I have driven down this

block a number of times since my family moved away in 1975, but
I haven't spent any time here for more than twenty years.

I pull my rental car up in front of the Galloway house and feel
surprise at how excited I am to be there, and how much I am
looking forward to again being inside someone's home on the
8900 block of Chappel.

Jeanine Galloway is an attractive woman in her mid-fifties
who is at first a little wary but then warms up rather quickly.
Once comfortable, Jeanine has a friendly but no-nonsense atti-
tude.

WILLIAM GALLOWAY

When Jeanine and I bought this house in April of 1968, we felt
like we were in Dreamland. We were only the second African-
American family on the block, but that didn't bother us. We loved
the house itself, and we fell in love with the whole area—we especially loved having Stony Island Park right across the street.

JEANINE GALLOWAY

And Bill was already teachin' at Bowen, so it was very convenient.

WILLIAM GALLOWAY

We were both teaching already, starting to build our careers; and
our first child was about to start school. So our attention was in-
ward, family oriented; and I think we saw those careers and this
house as places we would retire from.

JEANINE GALLOWAY

We'd been livin' in an apartment in the Chatham area while I finished my master's. It was all African-American there, and we
were all upwardly mobile—that was your rising middle class at
that point. Where I grew up, everybody was very much service
workers, basically. Now you'd call the area I grew up in the Black
Belt, but we didn't use that term then (*laughs*)—it was just our
neighborhood. And nowadays they'd probably say it was a

ghetto, but in my mind *ghetto* has a different connotation. But I never really came in contact with white people at all, basically, except in school. And you just knew that you could not go north of, you know, 63rd Street; you knew that you could not go east of Cottage Grove. All blacks just lived in that same, small area of the South Side.

WILLIAM GALLOWAY

There were actually racial covenants written into deeds in certain areas of Chicago prohibiting the selling of property to blacks *and* Jews until the late forties and early fifties when that sort of thing was made illegal.

JEANINE GALLOWAY

But we didn't know about that then. Living in a black neighborhood was just our reality. Chatham was only different in that it had nicer buildings than where I grew up, and there was that sense of bein' part of a rising African-American middle class.

Bill and I wanted to buy a house *there*, but people weren't moving. We only moved out here because we could *not* find a place in Chatham.

WILLIAM GALLOWAY

When we first moved to this area, there were little things about the neighborhood that I hadn't ever experienced anywhere else that are gone now—things I really loved. The fruit truck would come by during the summer selling fruit right from the farm. You could have orange juice delivered, or groceries, good-quality meat. You could have milk delivered—that was a real luxury.

JEANINE GALLOWAY

As black people, this was all totally unique to us.

WILLIAM GALLOWAY

You could have most anything delivered to your house, and this was *never* the case in any other neighborhood we lived in. (*laughs*)

LAWRENCE
Gerald and Linda Martin are a black couple in their late forties who live on Chappel across the street from my old house. The Martins and my family were neighbors for three years, but we never knew each other.

Linda is attractive—tall and full-figured—with a friendly face and manner that helps her past her initial nervousness in this situation. Her speech is deliberately paced but lively. Gerald is of medium height, thin, with chiseled features underneath a close-cropped beard. His speech rhythms are fast; his manner is sharp and to the point, and he stands throughout the conversation.

LINDA MARTIN
It was an impulsive move.

GERALD MARTIN
She was pregnant.

LINDA MARTIN
We were living in South Shore, and Gerald said that we weren't going to raise a baby in the apartment because it got cold up there sometimes. (*laughs*)

This was 1968. So we bought a house at the western edge of the neighborhood on Ridgeland, just this side of Stony Island Boulevard. It was a cute little doll house, but we called it our palace. We lived there till 1972 when we moved here to Chappel.

GERALD MARTIN
This neighborhood seemed clean, relatively safe—there didn't seem to be a lot of riffraff hangin' around.

LINDA MARTIN
Plus Gerald had a shoe store nearby in South Shore.

GERALD MARTIN

I was also goin' to business school at night, and Linda was gettin' her master's at DePaul.

LINDA MARTIN

I remember the day we were moving in—we must have been the second or third black family on that block. An older white gentleman from across the street came over and started telling us that his job moved out to some suburb, and he was sayin', "This commute is gettin' hard. I'll probably have to move close to my job." It was like he was saying, "I'm gonna be movin', but it's not because you're movin' in here," you know. (*laughs*) But I never really got to know any of the white families on Ridgeland.

GERALD MARTIN

Sometimes, coming and going, people would say hello to you.

LINDA MARTIN

But I can't remember anybody comin' over with the welcome wagon, or a cake, or a cup of sugar.

WILLIAM GALLOWAY

When we first moved here, some of the neighbors welcomed us onto the block; some ignored us.

JEANINE GALLOWAY

One family brought a nice gift for our daughter, which I still have. But I have to admit, I was surprised when individuals welcomed us. And after a while my perception was that the welcome couldn't have been all that genuine, because they did move.

But I never felt fearful movin' in here. It just didn't really occur to me that we would not be—I was gonna say *accepted*, but I guess it's more like *tolerated*. (*laughs*) I didn't think that people would throw things at us. See, you take a blue-collar neighborhood like Bridgeport, or Cicero—we knew we couldn't *go* out to those places. (*laughs*) They would, if you just *walked* out there, they would get violent, or run you back home. Out here I thought we would probably be ignored more than anything else.

LINDA MARTIN
I don't think it bothered me—not really being welcomed. I didn't expect that.

GERALD MARTIN
That was at the height of the black power movement, so there were a lot of conversations about pride, and we felt we had a right to be here.

LINDA MARTIN
It was our perception that the higher the socioeconomic status of the white community—if they didn't like blacks comin' in, they were just gonna move. If you have white people throwin' rocks and burnin' crosses on your lawn, that's because they're poor *(laughs)* and they can't go anywhere. So they're mad. They're gonna retaliate.

JEANINE GALLOWAY
Also at that time, I was not aware of all the different ethnic groups within the Caucasian race—basically, I guess it would be like thinking all blacks are the same thing. *(laughs)* But to me, if it wasn't black, it was white. Just white. So it wasn't until we were here a while, and with Bill teaching at Bowen High School, that I realized, for instance, that the Jewish people had been strong in this neighborhood.

LINDA MARTIN
When we found our first house, the realtor told us that the area a few blocks away was called Pill Hill because a lot of doctors lived up there—and in my mind that kind of went along with Jewish people. *(laughs)* And I also had this sense of Jewish people bein' connected with major black organizations like the NAACP or the Urban League—fighting for the rights of minorities. But still, I didn't move in here thinking of this as a Jewish

neighborhood. I didn't do a lot of separating of that then—a person was just white.

WILLIAM GALLOWAY

I had a different awareness than Jeanine of this being a Jewish community from teaching at Bowen, and I'd also had some positive contact with some Jewish people in my hometown of Racine, Wisconsin. So with my experiences, and knowing that blacks and Jews shared some similar experiences—you know, slavery, discrimination; we'd been partners in the civil rights struggle—I thought we had an awful lot in common. I was really surprised when certain things happened—like people leavin' the area—that showed a gap between the two groups.

GERALD MARTIN

When we moved into the area, I think I just assumed it wouldn't be long before it would be black. (*laughs*) According to the patterns in other Chicago neighborhoods, we knew that with blacks movin' in, most of the whites were gonna leave.

LINDA MARTIN

And it was beyond our control—if they were gonna move, they were gonna move.

GERALD MARTIN

You have to understand though, I wasn't thinkin' all that much about it. On some level that preceded conscious thinking, I—white people stayin' just seemed highly unlikely.

People were already startin' to make money by scarin' other people into sellin' their houses. And on another level, powerful forces like real estate interests and the government were puttin' money into buildin' up the suburbs after World War II—expressways were bein' built, and businesses were movin' out that way. I know they say the expressways were built for defense, but people were also bein' encouraged to move out to those areas; and with somethin' like five million black folk who had come north into the cities during and after World War II, they would be excep-

---

tional white people who would face all of that and say, "I'm not gonna move," (*laughs*) you know. Extremely exceptional. To me, this was definitely a neighborhood in transition.

WILLIAM GALLOWAY

To me, this was just a community, and I was gonna fit into it. See, in Racine there was a small African-American population there and we were accepted as part of the community. So I just thought we were moving into a neighborhood made up of people with a similar outlook, and that they would accept us as good people, that they'd accept us for who we were. We knew who we were.

JEANINE GALLOWAY

I never thought we would be viewed as individuals. I thought we would always be viewed as just black people; and I think blacks are always viewed—anything that's negative, they're viewed as a group. So when they see those of us who are tryin' to move away from—who don't really fit with certain stereotypes—I don't expect them to say, "Oh, they're all not like the people who were rioting on the West Side, or in Detroit. Maybe the other kind is in the minority." I just assume they think we're all like whatever you see on TV—the worst kind of whatever.

WILLIAM GALLOWAY

Between all the riots and the civil rights movement, the media at that time had a very negative image of blacks that was hard to fight. But I think what caused a huge shift in this neighborhood was Martin Luther King being assassinated. Those riots scared a lot of people. It tore Bowen High School apart for a while. No one around here had ever seen anything like it.

That was a scary time.

6

Riot, April 1968

JEANINE GALLOWAY
The time of the King riots was a dangerous time for African Americans in Chicago.

WILLIAM GALLOWAY
There was a lot of fear of police. They were stopping everybody. An individual's education and a profession were no protection.

LINDA MARTIN
The Illinois National Guard was right down in Jackson Park.

WILLIAM GALLOWAY
The National Guard was patrolling Stony Island Boulevard, and west to Cottage Grove.

JEANINE GALLOWAY
It was like an armed camp.

GERALD MARTIN
I can remember drivin' down Lake Shore Drive and traffic bein' real heavy that day, and then it dawned on me: people were tryin' to get outta the city—

RICHARD GOLD
A lot of parents kept their kids home from school the day after King was killed.

GERALD MARTIN
—particularly the white people, they were tryin' to get out early.

LAWRENCE
The administration of Warren Elementary told those of us who did go to school that Friday morning not to return after lunch. They told us to go home and stay inside, to stay off the streets.

RICHARD GOLD
There was talk that there was going to be rioting all over the South Side.

ARTHUR DREYER
63rd Street was set fire right away.

WILLIAM GALLOWAY
63rd Street, South Shore High School, 87th Street were burned or looted.

LINDA MARTIN
There were riots in a lot of areas. And in the schools—

JEANINE GALLOWAY
In the schools there was a lot of confusion. Where I was teachin', the kids were demonstratin'.

WILLIAM GALLOWAY
At Bowen—it was rough.

JANE WYSOCKER
At Bowen they told everybody to go home.

DANIEL MAYER
The gym teachers are walking through the halls, and the halls are pretty much deserted—there were no black people around—and the gym teachers are telling us, "Go home. Get the hell out of here. There's gonna be trouble."

JANE WYSOCKER
As I was leaving the building, I saw a lot of black kids marching around the school—

WILLIAM GALLOWAY
The black kids were demonstrating.

JANE WYSOCKER
—chanting about black power.

DANIEL MAYER
It was tense.

DARNELL WILSON
The Bowen student body was upset, because we asked for a memorial service to honor Dr. King, and we was told we could not have one. We had grown in numbers by then, but the administration still said no.

JANE WYSOCKER
At one point I remember I saw Darnell out there demonstrating, and I thought, "Some of these kids are my friends."

DARNELL WILSON
So at that time we took it upon ourself and we had some altercations.

DANIEL MAYER

I heard that within fifteen minutes they just started pouncing on any white people around.

DARNELL WILSON

It was almost like a major riot.

WILLIAM GALLOWAY

Kids were beating up on each other in the halls—black on white. I remember coming out of my classroom and separating two boys that I knew. The black kid was crying, and beating up on the other kid.

KEITH ROBERTS

That day was ugly. There was a sense that somebody had wronged us.

WILLIAM GALLOWAY

There was a lot of trashing of lockers, and stuff was thrown all over the halls.

KEITH ROBERTS

There were the mill kids, and some guys from Hirsch High School and CVS—they came over to our school and tried to start some shit. My friends and I, we weren't fightin' anybody. We were actually tryin' to protect anybody that we knew, keep them out of the way. 'Cause these other guys—they started a mini-riot.

DARNELL WILSON

I don't recall really seein' blacks jumpin' on whites. I think it was more verbal stuff goin' on.

KEITH ROBERTS

You had that herd mentality where they just wanted to jump on anybody white; and white kids *were* gettin' hit upside the head.

So now you have intervening groups of blacks sayin', *"No,* not this one. He's *okay."*

But you can't stop the herd, so your white friends are like, "What are you doin'?" And I'm like, "I'm tryin' to save you." And some black kids couldn't conceive of us havin' white friends, so when you did step in you became suspect. But everything happened so quick. Even Mexican guys were gettin' attacked, so there wasn't any rhyme or reason.

DARNELL WILSON

Then the administration panicked and called out the Police Department, called in the National Guard.

WILLIAM GALLOWAY

The police lined themselves up outside the school in riot gear.

JANE WYSOCKER

I was very upset—King being murdered was such an awful thing. And it scared me that police were all over the place.

DARNELL WILSON

I went out the side door of the school, and there was National Guard troops standing on the curb, almost shoulder to shoulder a few feet apart, all the way down to the bus stop.

JANE WYSOCKER

Police in riot gear—I'd never seen that before. I thought, "What's gonna happen?"

DARNELL WILSON

They told all us black kids to get on the bus and go back west toward Stony Island.

JANE WYSOCKER

I had never felt that kind of racial tension. But the black girls I knew from gym class were somewhat protective.

KEITH ROBERTS
My friends and I started walkin' people home—a group of us.

JANE WYSOCKER
They insisted on walking me home.

KEITH ROBERTS
We were maybe twenty-five people, and we were like this blob. As we went to you, you could become part of us and we'd protect you, because kids from CVS were just roamin' the neighborhood that day lookin' for shit.

WILLIAM GALLOWAY
There were kind of demarcation points in the neighborhood, and those were crossed, for instance, by CVS kids—

DARNELL WILSON
After the National Guard put us on those buses, a lot of the Bowen students met up with CVS students in Stony Island Park. And CVS was undergoing the same thing as Bowen that day, but their student population had more blacks. And at the same time South Shore High School had walked out and they was comin' our way up Jeffery Boulevard.

KEITH ROBERTS
There was rioting at South Shore.

DARNELL WILSON
So now you have the black student bodies from Bowen, CVS, and South Shore all converged up in Stony Island Park, and then they continued down 87th Street—

DANIEL MAYER
They ran riot.

DARNELL WILSON
Vandalizin' . . .

KEITH ROBERTS
They just kind of rampaged the whole area.

DANIEL MAYER
Smashing windows . . .

JEANINE GALLOWAY
Trashin' businesses—

DARNELL WILSON
Doin' a lot of destruction . . .

JEANINE GALLOWAY
Breakin' glass.

DANIEL MAYER
Looting everything . . .

DARNELL WILSON
. . . all the way from Jeffery . . .

DANIEL MAYER
from Jeffery west to Cottage Grove.

KEITH ROBERTS
They tore up everything in their path on the way home. There were no white people on the street at that point.

LAWRENCE
My parents kept me home all of that afternoon and evening. I was glad to be out of harm's way, but I was also terribly curious about what was going on in the neighborhood. I spent much of the day looking out our picture window hoping to catch a glimpse of something happening—anything—all to no avail. Our street remained eerily quiet.

DANIEL MAYER
Later that day I drove 87th Street to check out the damage.

KEITH ROBERTS

I was workin' at that time at Mr. D's on 87th with Darnell Wilson, and we were just amazed. Mr. D told us that he locked the door, and the kids whooped and hollered, and just tore things up, and whatever was there they took.

DANIEL MAYER

Anything that was a clothes or record or appliance store, stuff had been stolen.

KEITH ROBERTS

But none of the store owners that I knew got hurt. It was violent toward property, not toward people.

DANIEL MAYER

This drugstore where I worked wasn't damaged because the black guy who was the janitor stood out in front, and as the mob approached he'd tell the kids, "The man who owns this store is good people; he takes care of us," and they left the place untouched.

But the entire street for blocks—the windows were smashed, shattered glass everywhere. It was a mess.

ARTHUR DREYER

It was a shock wave.

LOUISE DREYER

My daughter was at Bowen that day—and I was a basket case until she got home.

SHIRLEY ADLER

I don't think I really began to think about moving until I sat in the beauty shop on 87th Street and watched them go down the street breaking windows.

JEROME ADLER

And even then we weren't ready to move yet.

Riot

LOUISE DREYER
People were just feeling that it was like what had happened the year before on the West Side—

WILLIAM GALLOWAY
The riots scared a lot of people.

LOUISE DREYER
There my father literally had a gun put to his head . . .

SHIRLEY ADLER
The rioting . . .

LOUISE DREYER
. . . and the fires . . .

SHIRLEY ADLER
Fear. It did put some fear into you.

KEITH ROBERTS
My friends and I weren't in between cultures that day. In one way we were almost empowered. See, we're *with* the blacks, but we're not beatin' up anybody—we're savin' people, but you know nobody's gonna mess with you.

LOUISE DREYER
I was scared. We weren't educated in living with this.

KEITH ROBERTS
It was a strange feeling.

JANE WYSOCKER
I don't remember the riots on 87th Street. I remember my own emotional state—

RICHARD GOLD
That was the only time the neighborhood ever felt unsafe or threatening.

JANE WYSOCKER

I felt horribly sad.

MARILYN KIER

The next day the JCC opened and people spoke to the kids about Martin Luther King, read poems, sang songs. . . .

JANE WYSOCKER

For the next few days, if you drove around you were supposed to turn your lights on or honk your horn, and that meant you were in sympathy.

MARILYN KIER

It was important to the black children that we were aware of the terrible tragedy that had happened to their people.

JANE WYSOCKER

Still, I remember carrying a wrench around in my purse for a few days, (*laughs*) as if I really needed it.

SHIRLEY ADLER

I became very aware that this neighborhood was just an island in the sea of the rest of the world, and it could be invaded.

JANE WYSOCKER

But by the time King was killed, I was close with my black friends again; the separatist thing they'd been going through wasn't standing between us anymore. Then after the riot there was all this new tension.

KEITH ROBERTS

None of my friends were part of the fightin', but white kids were lookin' at me that day like I was gonna do somethin' bad to them, and if I couldn't stop somebody else, their whole opinion changed. You could feel it in the next weeks as we tried to re-build.

JANE WYSOCKER

And you could see that everyone was really sad about the tension. You didn't want to feel estranged, but everyone kept their distance, in a protective way.

KEITH ROBERTS

Now, my close friends like Jane knew that nothin' had changed between us, but there were other folks who didn't know where you stood. They'd look at you like, "Were you one of the ones who were riotin'?"

DARNELL WILSON

I didn't break any windows—

KEITH ROBERTS

"Could it have been you, or you?"

DARNELL WILSON

I followed them down 87th Street, because I was headin' home—

KEITH ROBERTS

"Were you one of the ones that I heard about?"

DARNELL WILSON

—I was walkin' because the buses had stopped runnin'.

KEITH ROBERTS

So that changed the atmosphere around the school for the rest of the semester; and for some it was never repaired.

DARNELL WILSON

But I really didn't see no effect or tension afterward between the Jewish and the black kids. Like I said before, we both middle class or upper class, so you didn't have no problem. We blended. The harmony was there.

KEITH ROBERTS

The black kids who had been on the fringes of relationships with white kids probably felt the aftermath more than the rest of us. And some of them wanted to be badasses, or they wanted to pretend to be bad; so they never owned up to participatin', or disowned it.

That's how blacks are. We need a reputation because it makes you feel that you have something. Because almost everywhere you go, you have nothing. So if you get the reputation of being a badass just by not saying anything—"I'm a badass? Fine with me"—you can put the swagger on and people go, "I bet he was one of the ones."

See, bein' black is like havin' somethin' on your face that no one ever tells you is there. People look at you different all the time. It's like there is something always wrong with you. That's one feeling. The other feeling is that whatever happens black around the city, people think you know about it—you're somehow responsible for it. You're constantly being judged for something, and it's never positive.

WILLIAM GALLOWAY

As an African American, sometimes you feel that you're no more than a black box sitting over in the corner—(*pause*) without identity—or any importance for how you fit in, or are needed by the larger society. Just maybe tolerated, or depending on the mood of the society, maybe even wiped out. (*he takes a longer pause*) Some of our problems as a community, you could trace back to this great need to be accepted. If you don't feel that you're accepted, your self-image is not very positive, and you do the things that cause self-destruction.

DARNELL WILSON

So after Dr. King got killed, and after the vandalism of the business district, the neighborhood started changin'.

SHIRLEY ADLER

It started to feel like them and us.

WILLIAM GALLOWAY
That was a scary time.

DARNELL WILSON
All the Jewish people started movin'.

WILLIAM GALLOWAY
They saw South Shore change almost overnight.

DARNELL WILSON
That's when the flight started.

LOUISE DREYER
As far as the mass exodus in our neighborhood, that was the starting point; that was when the greater influx of those people began.

DANIEL MAYER
Yeah, the race was on after Martin Luther King was killed. The neighborhood was finished.

KEITH ROBERTS
From that day on, everything changed.

7

Flight, 1968–1969

LAWRENCE

*It was extraordinary to me that a riot could happen in our neigh-borhood—some of it right down the block at Stony Island Park.
Yet the event didn't frighten me or make me want to leave the
community. The riot had been provoked by a tragic circumstance;
I assumed that after the dust settled and the windows were re-placed, life on the South Side would return to normal.*

*But by the time I graduated from Warren Elementary School
two months later—June of '68—a fever was sweeping through the
community about moving. The air was ripe with rumors about
who was staying and who was leaving; and there was a lot of talk
among kids and their parents about how friendships were going
to be broken up, and how sad that was. That summer is when it
began to sink in for me that our neighborhood might really*

change, and I found myself drifting away from friends whom I knew were moving. My attitude was that if they were going, they might as well already be gone; and I took it as a matter of pride that my family was planning to stay.

LOUISE DREYER

It happened slowly, and then all of a sudden, *BOOM*—everyone was gone. Everything changed. Before you knew it, this one, that one. And then you heard, "So and so's moving." People didn't want to be the last.

MARILYN KIER

It was rapid. It was awful. As hard as we wanted to work to convince people that it was okay to live in an integrated area, it was astonishing to see the way a lot of people left. It was like a fire.

RICHARD GOLD

A significant number of our class bolted that summer after King was killed, so that they could start high school in the suburbs. And the next big dividing line was before our sophomore year— between those two summers we lost a lot of people.

MARILYN KIER

They were just going. They were out. It was really an exodus.

JANE WYSOCKER

I can't remember when the phone calls started, but the realtors started blockbusting, and it got worse and worse as time went on. They'd call every week and ask if we were interested in selling our house; they'd talk about property values and I'd hang up the phone on them.

SHIRLEY ADLER

The rioting. After that, even people who thought they would stay decided it was time to go. And there was a fear about the education. The reason you always got was that they had to find good schools for their kids.

RICHARD GOLD

People kept talking about the education getting worse at Bowen—which is interesting, because our first year there the school was basically as good as it was when my brother had entered three years earlier; and the ethnic and racial mix still seemed fairly healthy.

Nevertheless, the main topic of conversation that I can remember around my house during those two years was, "Now who's moving?"

JANE WYSOCKER

For a while some people were resisting leaving. I remember signs in front of some houses that said, "This house is *not* for sale." But blockbusters were not only calling you, they'd knock on your door, and if you said your house wasn't for sale, they'd tell you why it should be.

JEROME ADLER

There was panic selling. A lot of people felt that if they went fast they wouldn't lose their money. And certainly some of it was, "I'll live with some of them, but I'll be damned if I'll live on a block where they're all black." It was an "I don't want to be the last one off the boat" sort of feeling.

ARTHUR DREYER

There was never panic selling, and never a mass exodus. No. It was a block-by-block thing.

LOUISE DREYER

Well, no, don't forget—no—it went block by block, but also—

ARTHUR DREYER

Values remained fairly constant. Nobody got rich off their house, but everybody got their money out.

LOUISE DREYER

But also, I can well remember how upset we were every time a family moved out. My feeling was that if everybody had hung in, we might have been living on an island . . . but at least we would have all been together. But every day you'd find out—people were moving out in the middle of the night.

MARILYN KIER

Some of my friends, "Oh, we're not moving," then the next thing you knew they were packing up. It was a joke. These were people who thought blacks were undesirable, or they had bad associations from the way some other neighborhoods—the West Side, for instance—had changed and then deteriorated.

JEROME ADLER

It was like sitting around with a big group—"Okay, guys, in the next year, we're all going."

SHIRLEY ADLER

It was who found a house first. . . .

JEROME ADLER

Exactly. And we all went.

MARILYN KIER

They practically gave away some of the houses.

JANE WYSOCKER

I spent that summer of '68 thinking, "The world has gone crazy." Martin Luther King had been killed, and then Bobby Kennedy; my friends in the antiwar movement were getting the shit kicked out of them in Grant Park at the Democratic Convention; and now people were fleeing from our neighborhood in droves because blacks were moving in. I remember that all I kept thinking to myself was, "The world has gone crazy. The world has gone crazy."

Flight

LAWRENCE

The flight disgusted me; and though I knew it wasn't just Jews who were leaving, I didn't care about the rest of the community— my anger was with the Jewish community. The flight ran counter to all the moral teaching the community had offered, teaching I had swallowed whole. It ran counter to my own positive experience with certain black individuals. And nothing I was hearing at home was abating the anger. From my parents' point of view, the Jews were running because they did not want to live with the "schvarzes."

KEITH ROBERTS

Boy, the summer after those riots, you could see the families movin' out. You could see the breakup of friendships. And I knew I wasn't goin' anywhere, so it was like, "What do you mean you're goin'? Where are you goin'?" "We're goin' to Homewood." "We're goin' to Flossmoor." "We're goin' to Glencoe." "We're goin' to Winnetka." It was as if my white friends were bein' yanked away when they didn't want to go. I can remember the girls cryin' as they explained it to their girlfriends. Jane and I used to have conversations about, "Why couldn't it be different?"

DARNELL WILSON

It was everybody. It seemed like it was all the white people leavin'—Jewish people, Irish people, Polish, Serbian—the whole nine yards. I couldn't understand it. If you have a home, and you have a community, and you have businesses there, where you goin'? I was raised that we was all people and everything was fine. So I kept tryin' to figure out, "Are you movin' because you don't want to be around black people? Okay. But wherever you go you gonna be around black people."

KEITH ROBERTS

I didn't want the neighborhood to change, but there was nothin' you could do about it. The whole area where I lived by Stony Island Boulevard was gettin' to be all black.

DARNELL WILSON

I was like, "Why are you leavin'? Nobody's not gonna do nothin' to you. I'm not gonna break into your garage and steal your lawn mower. We got two lawn mowers, okay?" Then some of the parents didn't want the black guys and the Jewish girls gettin' together, and I was like, what kinda sense does that make? If they like each other, they like each other. So what?

WILLIAM GALLOWAY

I think our street changed more gradually than the neighborhood as a whole.

JEANINE GALLOWAY

Our children played with a couple of white children on the block, and they were just like family.

WILLIAM GALLOWAY

Parents were uprooting that, tearing that apart. At one point people were moving out overnight.

JEANINE GALLOWAY

At four in the mornin'.

WILLIAM GALLOWAY

(*laughing*) Now, that was something different.

JEANINE GALLOWAY

When we first moved in, Bill and I would say to each other, "We're only two families on this block. If the white people stay here, it won't ever turn black." That's what always struck me as so silly. It will only turn black if you let it; if you leave. But then, when the change took place, the individuals that were movin' in were just as nice as the ones who were leavin', so it didn't seem to make any difference. As our daughter once said, "Well, I lost one friend . . ."

122

Flight

WILLIAM GALLOWAY
—"and I got another one."

LINDA MARTIN
It was like the white families where we first lived over on Ridge-land just kind of stole away in the night. We talked about that. "Yep. Another one's gone."

GERALD MARTIN
It's hard for me to even remember a lot of (*laughs*) white people bein' around. I don't have much memory of that. But, on the other hand, I didn't take white folks leavin' personally. I always figured that the neighborhood would change to all black folk anyway, and that the people who would follow would be people of similar values and aspirations, and that the neighborhood would only get better.

LINDA MARTIN
But those houses on Ridgeland turned like that (*snapping her fingers*).

WILLIAM GALLOWAY
And I think we all got manipulated for various people's gains.

JEANINE GALLOWAY
Obviously the real estate people made money, whites *and* blacks, with all this property changing hands.

WILLIAM GALLOWAY
And we saw how the white community was being barraged by the panic peddlers. Some of the literature was very derogatory. But then a lot of what was goin' on was unspoken.

See, when we moved in, Jeanine and I went to some block meetings, and people were saying all the right things about integration; but afterward we would try to guess which families would be the next ones to leave. And I became pretty familiar with, you know, the excuses I got from neighbors for why they

123

were moving—and I remember this one woman got up at a meeting and said, "I don't want to live by the park any longer," and I turned to my wife and said, "Is our name Park?"

MARILYN KIER

There were some very volatile meetings at the JCC at that time, and also with the PTA. There were people who were very angry. I remember one meeting at our synagogue where some man called my husband and I, quote, "my nigger-loving friends." This was an issue—some people considered us these kooky, liberal people because an integrated world was the one we wanted to live in.

WILLIAM GALLOWAY

And then we attended some SECO meetings—that was the Southeast Community Organization, but those meetings were more about keeping the community safe and maintaining neighborhood services.

JEANINE GALLOWAY

And property values.

WILLIAM GALLOWAY

I don't really recall any serious discussion at those meetings about the upheaval that was goin' on.

ARTHUR DREYER

We started SECO. It was a grassroots organization with delegates from all the neighborhood churches and synagogues, and from a couple of banks. There were mass meetings where we consistently had over a thousand people. I would say less than 10 percent were Jewish. The goals were to maintain property values, maintain stability. It wasn't about achieving integration. And it worked, in terms of buying time and averting a real selling panic.

LOUISE DREYER

But integration was not the goal. There was no organized outreach to try to create an integrated community.

ARTHUR DREYER

No—no effort like that of any sort.

JEROME ADLER

There was a ton of effort made to reach out and stabilize that community. SECO, for example—it was the so-called leadership from the community, trying to maintain the *value* of it. We met up the wazoo. The feeling was that if integration was gonna come, let it come, but in a gradual, organized way. But it was my sense then, and it still is now, that the majority of blacks that moved into that community were not interested in living in an integrated—

SHIRLEY ADLER

They told you outright that it was your problem, not theirs. They didn't care. The history of the black community in Chicago has always been: there's a white community, they move in, and then resegregate it into a black community. SECO was trying to avoid that.

JEROME ADLER

One of the goals of SECO *was* integration. No question. But also, SECO was a totally white-run organization trying to get white people to stay, and the blacks weren't gonna try to manage it— they were just gonna let it flow.

The movement of the black community south was like *lava.*

WILLIAM GALLOWAY

One thing SECO was not about was trying to accomplish integration.

JEANINE GALLOWAY

No, nothin' like that. But you have to remember that I was raised around all black people anyway, so my feelings were different from Bill's in that I was not looking for an integrated area. I just wanted a nice place to settle and raise our children. Period. So it didn't matter to me, one way or the other, if the white people stayed or left. I would have hoped that, you know, we could have gotten along, and I think we could have; because, had they stayed, they would have probably seen that we were just like they were. But integration wasn't a goal I had in mind when we chose this neighborhood.

JEROME ADLER

It wasn't just SECO. I served on various committees, and you'd be meeting with people all the time about how to maintain the community, or how to make the racial balance work. But the blacks that moved into that area were militant. They absolutely didn't want an integrated community.

SHIRLEY ADLER

They wouldn't assimilate with us once they were in the majority. When a group becomes the majority, the minority is out; and we were the minority.

JEROME ADLER

Look, there was never an attempt for me to become buddies with the black people on our block—but I'd just as soon have lived in a community that's an integrated kind of world.

LINDA MARTIN

I don't think integration was the goal. The mere fact that we lived next door to each other made it integrated. That's all. But we didn't have all that much in common.

I think when black people move in somewhere, they don't necessarily feel they need to be the ones to reach out and say we're going to be good neighbors to you. I think we feel that if you are accepting of us, it is up to you to let us know that, and if you aren't, then we'll know that too. But integration wasn't our issue—we were movin' in. We always thought it was their problem. Our thought was more, "Why would they want to leave a nice neighborhood?"

GERALD MARTIN

You're thinkin' more about who's gonna move next door to you; and there are black people that I don't want to live next to, or that don't want to live next to me.

LINDA MARTIN

(*intensely*) But you take it personally that somebody doesn't want to live next to you *because* you're black.

I think subconsciously I always felt we weren't a wanted race, that it didn't matter what you looked like, how you sounded, whether you were intelligent or educated—you just weren't wanted, collectively. I think black people struggle with that feeling from birth to death.

So when I saw that the Jewish people were leaving this neighborhood, I wasn't surprised—but I was disappointed they went so fast.

GERALD MARTIN

You thought about that?

LINDA MARTIN

I did. But I thought it proved that given a choice, every ethnic group wants to live with their own. You had to work with other people, but you didn't have to live together, or even socialize. We weren't comfortable with it. It just didn't feel natural.

GERALD MARTIN

Black folks needed an expansion of their community. If there was a goal other than personal goals, *that* was it. I think some communities make a big effort to maintain a certain racial balance, but I never saw this community doin' that. I saw people not carin' if their white neighbors wanted to stay—and I don't know that it mattered that much. Our concerns were with the everyday struggle of livin' and maintainin' a decent neighborhood.

Personally, I don't see integration bein' that important to me. I see it bein' important to me that I can achieve the goals that I have for myself, and for my family, and that others should have the same right. My neighbor can be white next door—I don't want to live in his house. I want to live in my own house; and we may not like the same things—that's all right. I don't want to be fearful of the fact that we're different. And there's no need for him to be fearful either. But fear gets planted. Real estate, jobs, housing—see, racism is a very, very profitable business.

WILLIAM GALLOWAY
For me, the flight was a real eye-opener. Having grown up in Racine, a lot of this we never even discussed. Whites and blacks just lived together. To come to a larger metropolitan area and be more pigeonholed, I felt like it was taking me backward. I found it confining. It took a great deal of adjustment on my part to get used to it.

I never have gotten used to it.

8

Carrying On, 1969–1970

LAWRENCE
*The first wave of leaving was in full flight my freshman year at
Bowen, but it wasn't a subject I dwelled on. High school was a
whole new environment to explore, and though my friends were
still primarily Jewish, my world was suddenly a much more diverse place, black and white, Jewish and Gentile. Two places
where this was particularly evident were Stony Island Park,
where my new obsession with playing basketball was in full
bloom, and the Jewish Youth Center in nearby South Shore,
where I was part of a racially mixed theatre group. The shows
there were cast in a completely color-blind manner based purely
on talent, and the productions were terrific. But I think what I
most loved about this group were the huge parties we'd have on
Saturday nights after a performance. There would be fifty, sixty*

people, lots of music, dancing, enough beer to fill a swimming pool—and no racial tension of any kind that I can recall.

But after my freshman year—the summer of '69—the Youth Center shut down the program. Most of the Jewish kids in the group had graduated that June, and the center wasn't going to fund something that was servicing a primarily non-Jewish population.

KEITH ROBERTS

When we came back in the fall of '68, there were more blacks at Bowen, and the blacks that we started to get were more Afrocentric in nature. I became the head of the Afro History Club, and I got suspended from Bowen for requesting that we get Afro-American History classes—the suspension was because we orchestrated a walkout.

DANIEL MAYER

There was a definite attitude change in the black students at Bowen after King was killed. They were no longer Negro students—they were black students, they were in the Afro-American Club, and they were wearing Afros and African clothes. It was great to witness. I stayed friends with these kids. That didn't change.

KEITH ROBERTS

Also, the blacks that were comin' in at this point were not accustomed to whites. They looked at blacks who had white friends like, "How do you do this? We're not supposed to do this. What do you see in them?" So guys like Darnell and me had to say, "This is how it works here," and we're goin' around vouchin' for people, but the process keeps gettin' harder because the white people we're vouchin' for are leavin' so rapidly.

And this was also the time when South Side gangs were on the rise. You had the Egyptian Lords comin' out of Hirsch, the Blackstone Rangers comin' out of 63rd Street . . .

DANIEL MAYER

There were two big gangs, the Blackstone Rangers and the Devil's Disciples. The Rangers wore black berets, and the Disciples wore red berets.

KEITH ROBERTS

A lot of the CVS kids were joinin' the gangs, but guys at Bowen weren't in the gangs, though some of them were pretendin' to be—you know, wantin' to be badasses.

DANIEL MAYER

I remember that one time I took the wrong bus home from downtown and ended up at 63rd and Stony. When I realized where I was—which was right in the middle of Blackstone Ranger territory—I got really scared. So I went over to this gas station and told the attendant that I was lost, and at first he just kind of looked at me like, "You sure are, motherfucker, you sure are."

KEITH ROBERTS

I had my first gun pulled on me at the El at 47th Street because I wasn't in a gang. They were lookin' for a password, and I didn't know the word. Luckily a woman was walkin' by and said, "Hey, he's just a kid. Leave him alone." I was like, "Whoa." You know, your life passes before you. But I never saw any of that stuff around our neighborhood.

JANE WYSOCKER

One of my best friends was very badly beaten and left on a street in South Shore by some Rangerettes—it was really awful. So even though the gangs weren't in our neighborhoods, we knew about this sort of thing, and it caused a certain amount of tension.

LAWRENCE

At the end of my freshman year there was a gang-related shooting in the lunchroom at Bowen. Some kid walked in and killed another kid with a sawed-off shotgun. Everyone dove under the ta-

bles. The shooting was supposedly over some Latino drug dispute between two South Chicago gangs, but no one knew for sure. Nothing like that had happened at Bowen before. From then on, the lunchroom always had an armed guard.

DANIEL MAYER

And then I left for college in the fall of '69, but I'd come home all the time, and spend the summers there. Our area wasn't dangerous. And even though most of my friends were in the suburbs by then, I liked the fact that my family was still living on the South Side, that my parents were living in an integrated neighborhood. They stayed until 1975, at which point they retired to San Diego.

You know, a memory that I am glad to have is how nauseated my mother and father were at all the people who were splitting. They found it sickening. I used to brag to people that my parents didn't run.

LAWRENCE

My father would sometimes get very worked up over the subject of people leaving, and say things like, "All it took to get it going, Larry, was just one family. As soon as one moves, bingo, then everybody, they all just blow and blow and blow. It breaks your heart. If only they would stay still. So what if some black families come in. So what?"

My mother seemed more stunned than anything by how quickly the neighborhood was changing. One night at dinner she got a phone call from a friend, and then suddenly let out a cheer. It seemed that one of the first families to leave the neighborhood had moved out to an expensive southern suburb, and shortly after settling in they were greeted by some new neighbors—a black family—who were moving in next door.

RICHARD GOLD

I was depressed our sophomore year—so many people had left by then. I felt abandoned. That whole period of time from the fall of

'69 to the summer of '70 is a blur to me. Only a few of our old crowd were left; our AZA was evaporating. You were on Bowen's basketball team at that point, so I wasn't seeing you much. It was more like, "Wow, everybody's gone."

And I knew that my family wasn't going anywhere. I think my parents positively valued staying; but truthfully, we couldn't afford to move. Now to me, it wasn't a huge deal. Bowen was a lonelier place at that point, but I never perceived it as more dangerous. But I was worried that my parents and my younger sister would be stranded in this new environment after I went off to college, and it seemed there was no way out.

The interesting thing is we had become friends with the black family that moved in next door, and they were wonderful people. I remember sharing stuff—deciding who was going to paint the fence, that sort of thing. They were a definite improvement over the prior occupants.

KEITH ROBERTS

My senior year—I graduated June of '70—that was a great time. The distance that had set in between some of the black and white kids at Bowen after the riot finally got bridged, because we all got into that flower-power thing.

JANE WYSOCKER

We organized one sit-in where there was a whole assembly hall full of people, black kids and white kids, all protesting some problem we had with the school. The administration got nervous and tried to twist the problem into a black/white thing, and we turned that back on them by purposefully sitting there together with our arms around each other, so that when they would come in and talk about the racial differences, we were like, "What racial differences?" (*laughs*)

Around that time we also did a big show at the school that pulled a whole group of us together. It was an integrated cast, and we hung out together all year; and we actually spent a lot of time talking about race. We felt like we were learning to live together, work together, be together; and that's when we all had this dream that this was the way it would be in the future, and we would make it change.

This was the time Keith and I really got involved. We sort of were together our senior year, and stayed together through the summer.

KEITH ROBERTS

Jane and I had to maintain a certain amount of secrecy about our relationship—you don't know how people are gonna respond. I don't mean our close friends, but a lot of people definitely did not know. I don't know if her parents—I'm sure her parents knew, but they probably didn't want to know so they never said. It was one of those things.

JANE WYSOCKER

My father had once said that he would disown me if I ever went out with a black guy. He might have said that in the heat of an argument, but I took the statement seriously enough not to tell my folks what I was doing.

KEITH ROBERTS

My mother knew, and she was okay with it. But I don't know if a lot of black kids knew, because that part of society was so split. See, people like Jane and me, we were in the middle. We were goin' to Sly and the Family Stone concerts in Grant Park, to symphony concerts at Ravinia—we'd go out to the suburbs and visit our friends who had moved. The black fringe wouldn't be doin' any of that; they'd stay around Stony Island. And the white fringe would never leave the suburbs. But I was used to always negotiating between the white and the black worlds, so my relationship with Jane was no different.

JANE WYSOCKER

Keith and I used to like to go around the University of Chicago in

Hyde Park, because we could walk down the street there and people wouldn't stare at us like they would in our neighborhood. Once in a while we'd go over to his neighborhood, but we couldn't spend too much time there either, because I think he worried about what the neighbors would think.

It was serious between us—but everything was serious then. Everything was very important. I was in tears for most of the summer after I graduated. You're at that age when life is very dramatic. We were very old—we were much older then than we are now. (*laughs*)

KEITH ROBERTS

With Jane was where I could be real. But there was a melancholy side to our bein' together, because we knew that we weren't gonna get married even though we might have wanted to—see, my family would have been okay with it, but it would have been too much of a problem for hers. So we spent whatever time together we could, and we offered each other solace; but we knew, almost like the inevitability of people movin' away—it was just a matter of when.

JANE WYSOCKER

And then I went away to college and fell in love with someone else. I don't think it was because I decided that Keith and I was a relationship that couldn't happen—I just fell in love with someone else. But I never really fell out of love with Keith. And our friendship was very, very strong, so that's what remained, that deep understanding and acceptance of each other. We were soul mates—which probably makes it better that I don't see him very often.

KEITH ROBERTS

Nobody wanted Jane and me to be together—in a utopian sense they say they do, but when you attempt to get together, they attempt to break you apart. So I saw us goin' our separate ways off to college as a continuation of the breakup of the neighborhood, and I wasn't lookin' forward to that.

JANE WYSOCKER
I asked him once what happened with us—because before I left for college I was ready to run away with him and get married, and let my parents disown me. And I think chances are, if he had pushed a little, I might have gone ahead with it—I don't know. But his response was—

KEITH ROBERTS
"Reality set in."

JANE WYSOCKER
He looked at things from different angles. I was more of a dreamer. I could be very naive and say, "We'll just be happy—to hell with the rest of the world." And what was ironic was that my parents knew he was my friend, and they really liked him. I'd say to him, "Doesn't it make you crazy that my parents can't know about our relationship simply because of what you are?" And he'd say . . .

KEITH ROBERTS
"Yeah, but that's the way it is."

9

Disintegration, 1970–1971

LAWRENCE

*My friend Ron Mazur and I made Bowen's junior varsity basket-
ball team in the fall of 1969, the beginning of our sophomore
year. The racial composition of the team was sixty-forty black and
white. The coach—a white math teacher who was trying his hand
at coaching—was a nice fellow but ineffectual, and it wasn't long
before the varsity coach, John Nowicki, was supervising our
practices.*

*Nowicki seemed quickly to decide that Ron and I were the two
most capable players on the squad, and he often used us to
demonstrate the fundamentals he wanted everybody to learn.
That might not have been a problem except for the fact that Nowicki was foul-mouthed and somewhat of a bully, and in the
process he usually belittled the other players—especially the
black guys—for not being more like us. I was fifteen years old at*

the time, and the racial put-down that came through in his re-marks and his attitude was obvious to me—so I know it didn't go unnoticed among the black players, though none of us ever talked about it.

Once the season began, Ron and I were the only white players on the starting five, but we seemed to be the unofficial floor lead-ers, and the team got off to a decent start. Then, seemingly out of nowhere, Nowicki demanded that Ron cut his shoulder-length hair. Ron refused, and Nowicki immediately threw him off the team. No discussion. I tried to intervene, but both of them were too stubborn to be reasoned with.

I was now the only white guy on the starting five, and though I was among the team leaders in scoring to that point, no one would pass me the ball. When things went wrong on the court, all fingers pointed in my direction. On more than one occasion I al-most came to blows with a couple of my own teammates in prac-tice because they didn't like my physical style of play. Everyone knew what was going on—the black guys resented me for the way I'd been singled out for praise, and now that my partner was gone, I had no one watching my back and I would have to pay. Our math teacher-coach, being so far out of his depth, was help-less to affect the situation.

The split between us all became painfully obvious when, with eight seconds left on the clock against Hirsch High School, and our team down by one point, I sank a jump shot from the top of the key to win the game. Feeling the joy of the victory, my team-mates came rushing over to me, but at the last possible moment, still a few feet apart, we all seemed to look in each other's eyes and freeze. I remember I was thinking, "I know who you are; I know how we really feel about each other. Let's not pretend we're teammates. Fuck you." And to me, the looks on their faces seemed to be saying the same thing. So instead of embracing and celebrating, we all just turned and walked our separate ways back to the locker room.

From that point on the situation only got worse. I felt a lot of pressure to perform on those rare moments when the ball found its way into my hands, and I stopped playing with the same confidence I had played with at the start of the season. Publicly I never let on to my teammates how I was feeling. Privately the conflict had a devastating emotional impact on me. I remember sitting in the math teacher's car and releasing a season's worth of frustration by crying my eyes out. I had never before been around teammates who didn't act like teammates; I wasn't mature enough to know how to handle the situation, and the racial basis of the problem was the most disturbing thing of all because it seemed to create an impenetrable barrier.

I harbored serious dreams at the start of that season of going on to play college basketball, and maybe even becoming a coach. By season's end I had lost a lot of my enthusiasm for the organized game. It wasn't fun. My heart was no longer in it.

SHIRLEY ADLER
You have to understand my background. I went to the University of Chicago. I was a *real* liberal. I knew the struggle of the blacks. One of our closest friends from optometric school was a black man. When the first black moved onto my street—

JEROME ADLER
Our friend said, "Move. Get out."

SHIRLEY ADLER
He was a black guy who wouldn't live in a black community.

JEROME ADLER
His commentary was, "There will be a time in a few years when the neighborhood will be overrun and you won't be able to deal with them."

SHIRLEY ADLER
So, I was a liberal, and I became . . .

JEROME ADLER

. . . a bigot.

SHIRLEY ADLER

I became a bigot. (*they both laugh, a bit embarrassed*) There's nothing worse than a converted liberal. I felt everything I loved was being taken from me.

JEROME ADLER

The community was disappearing, and you felt, in some respects, they were taking that away from you.

SHIRLEY ADLER

I'm not a bigot in a true sense.

JEROME ADLER

Yes, you are.

SHIRLEY ADLER

I'm not going to swear and use derogatory terms—but I resented the fact that I was being forced out of the community. It really disturbed me. And I was angry at the black community that was making me move. I didn't have a big house—I truly loved the community. And I think I'm not such a liberal anymore.

LOUISE DREYER

I grew up in an area of Chicago which wasn't all Jewish, but it was all white. So I never had any experience with black people until things started with our neighborhood, and the West Side riots when my dad had a gun put to his head, and the King riots and the destruction on 87th Street. (*to her husband*) And then you were running into problems with the business being robbed and vandalized. I mean, when I really came to the point of loathing them was when we went through the final stages of having to give up the store, when five nights in a row, at two o'clock in the morning, we got a phone call that they were breaking in and our windows were shattered. I remember that last night, getting the same phone call and you sitting up on the side of the bed and just screaming. That was it. I wanted you out of there. I mean, I had gotten to the point where, I hate to say it, I was very prejudiced. They were coming in and they were taking my home, taking our business.

ARTHUR DREYER

But there were black people who were very supportive of us. I was taking courses at City College and I had a lot of black friends.

LOUISE DREYER

That's true. I was putting them all together. But it was very traumatic to me. I resented terribly that they were coming into *my home*.

ARTHUR DREYER

For me, it was intimidating to go from being a respected member of the business community in South Shore to an outsider—and that's basically what happened. My roots were deep there—the chamber of commerce, officer in the Kiwanis, a director of the South Shore Bank. But by the late sixties this was all finished for me. The business was suffering financially, and then there were all the burglaries, broken windows . . .

LOUISE DREYER

A friend of ours owned a business at 61st and Halsted that had been there for forty years, and he told us they came up to him and said, "We're your partners, and if you don't make us your partners . . ." So he just closed up. And those who were forced out of business, or approached that way, developed such a hatred for the blacks. . . .

ARTHUR DREYER

(*becoming uncomfortable*) They weren't the majority. This was one small segment; but one feeds on another, and for a million reasons, it all goes.

JEROME ADLER

So from 1968 to 1970 was about introspection among the people who were left. We could see the handwriting on the wall. People became realistic, and I think a little more self-interested. The question changed from "Should we leave?" to "Where should we go, and what do we do with the synagogue? We could sell the property, eliminating the mortgage, and still have 200,000 bucks left over. Or should we all try to go somewhere with our temple?" Chicago communities have done that for years.

SHIRLEY ADLER

But there was a disagreement between those of us who wanted to move the synagogue to the southern suburbs and those who wanted to go north.

JEROME ADLER

And Rabbi Steinman wasn't like Aaron Fineman. He wasn't the kind of strong leader that people would follow.

SHIRLEY ADLER

And Steinman didn't want to start over.

JEROME ADLER

The thing is, *I* didn't want to start over. I had already spent a dozen years of my life bustin' my head against the wall and I really, truly didn't want to go start a congregation from scratch and build it again.

See, unofficially, I was the last president of the shul—the president was ill—and I was also pretty much chairman of the dissolution committee. So if I wanted to take all the money and move the congregation south, I had enough votes to do it. But it would have meant a really big push on my part.

Disintegration

ARTHUR DREYER

I think Jerry Adler had the idea that he wanted to be *the* last president of the congregation. You know—after him, the deluge.

LOUISE DREYER

And he wanted every artifact in the building to go to some shul in the south suburbs. He had his hands—I was the last sisterhood president—and he had his hands on the charter, was walking out the back door with it, and I walked up to him and said, "I beg your pardon, but that belongs to *me.*" (*Louise again points to the charter, framed and hanging on their den wall*)

ARTHUR DREYER

I don't know why it belonged to you. . . .

LOUISE DREYER

Because I was one of the twelve original families. Listen, I had been suffering enough, watching everything else coming off the walls. I wasn't letting him get it. I mean, this man—he wasn't fit to wash anybody's—he wanted to be the big cheese. He and his friends wanted to be the all-important ones and decide to dissolve the synagogue or not to dissolve.

ARTHUR DREYER

Cliques are always part of Jewish life.

LOUISE DREYER

And I got my hands on that charter by sheer—I just grabbed it.

JEROME ADLER

So we sold the building to the Board of Education and it became a magnet school. And then we distributed the money, the books, the torahs, the plaques—it all went to various synagogues around the city.

LOUISE DREYER

I think we gave away about $150,000 altogether.

ARTHUR DREYER
We closed the doors in 1970.

SHIRLEY ADLER
My son was one of the last Bar Mitzvahs there.

JEROME ADLER
May of '70.

SHIRLEY ADLER
We were already living out here, but we went back for the Bar Mitzvah.

LOUISE DREYER
I was so traumatized by it all. As I was walking out of the building for the last time, the cantor tried to console me. He said, "Look at it this way, everything we had here will now be used to try and seed good Jewish life somewhere else."

At that moment I wasn't so easily consoled.

WILLIAM GALLOWAY
I felt abandoned by the Jewish people. We were a people reaching out—a community reaching out to another community that had some common experiences. We wanted to be accepted, to establish a base, interact with our neighbors. At first I couldn't understand why people were moving out so suddenly. It was like having a tooth pulled for no reason. And then I couldn't understand why people *kept* leaving, why the individuals who didn't leave right away couldn't see that those of us moving in were at the same economic level—that we had similar values. . . .

JEANINE GALLOWAY
It wasn't like this area was attractin' lower-income-type people. It wasn't like some other areas where big apartments were gettin' cut up into a lot of little ones. This area is single-family houses. We were heavily screened by the realtors and the banks—

Disintegration

WILLIAM GALLOWAY

We could have been rejected for a variety of bogus reasons. But we liked the screening—it prevented people from buying houses who couldn't afford them, who wouldn't have been able to afford to keep them up.

JEANINE GALLOWAY

So obviously there was some other problem. I just thought maybe it was the same old thing—when blacks move in, the property values decrease; or somebody might want to marry your daughter, the interracial thing. Because I had never lived around blacks who accost you on the street.

WILLIAM GALLOWAY

And those of us who moved here, we had to answer some questions too, from the members of our own community, you know— "What did you expect moving in there, that the whites would stay?"

LAWRENCE

Around the time the synagogue was closing—the spring of 1970—my parents put the choice to me as to whether we would stay in the neighborhood or move to the southern suburbs. I was completing my sophomore year at Bowen, and they were worried about how well I'd survive the next two years. They both have a vivid memory of me saying that if they were moving for my sake, don't do it.

I didn't want to leave. I'd been offered an important role on Bowen's varsity squad for the next year, and I wanted to see that opportunity through. I was also proud we had stayed, and I saw nothing to be gained by moving. My impression of the southern suburbs from the kids I knew who lived out there was that of a vast, drug-infested emptiness, a desolate life that held no promise of tangible improvement over the coming desolation on the South Side.

145

The South Side

RICHARD GOLD

We moved to Skokie in August of 1970. I believe that my mother never would have left the neighborhood out of loyalty as long as the synagogue was open, because that was her lifeline. But once it closed, the idea that we could live there without it was to her inconceivable.

I felt sad that we were leaving, but I was also relieved. I didn't think we'd ever get out of there. I still don't know how they did it financially.

JANE WYSOCKER

My family left in the summer of 1970, right after I graduated. I hated that we were leaving. But by that summer all of my parents' friends and family had left the South Side. Also, my folks were getting worried about safety because my mother didn't drive. When it reached the point where she was the only white person on the Stony Island bus, she decided it was time to go.

I felt a definite sense of pride about the fact that we hadn't run away, that I finished high school there. That's part of what was so hard about leaving.

It was very sad.

JEROME ADLER

See, my youngest daughter was only in fourth grade in 1969, and she was—

SHIRLEY ADLER

She was the only white girl left in her class.

JEROME ADLER

So we felt, "Enough is enough. Fifty-fifty we don't mind—living in an integrated community. But after that, forget it."

SHIRLEY ADLER

And our children had some experiences—our daughter was selling Girl Scout cookies and had the money taken from her. Things like that. 'Cause I wasn't looking to run away.

JEROME ADLER
Black kids would come and they'd stand on your lawn and—

SHIRLEY ADLER
—and sort of taunt you. (*shrugging it off*) Kids are kids.

JEROME ADLER
Did they get that at home, this, "Why don't you just leave, whitey?"

SHIRLEY ADLER
Not respecting your property.

JEROME ADLER
Hey—(*he whistles*) who needs this? Look, I fought for the temple, I fought with SECO—"Hey, you know what, hey, I did the best I could. It's time to go."

SHIRLEY ADLER
No guilt.

JEROME ADLER
Not a guilty feeling. I fought the good fight. I couldn't stay there with my three kids—my oldest was only fourteen at the time. I made a judgment. I did the best I could.

SHIRLEY ADLER
I didn't sneak out. I stayed almost till the bitter end. The synagogue was gone.

JEROME ADLER
Your friends are gone, you're not comfortable. Part of it may be fear. Part of it is "I'm isolated. Why do I need this? Why am I knockin' my head against the wall?"

SHIRLEY ADLER

I felt traumatized about moving.

JEROME ADLER

The last feeling I had was, "The people moving on my block don't want me to stay." That's how it felt. See, even out here—there are orientals, Indians, blacks on this block—that's not a problem, because it isn't a situation where every single person on the block but you is . . . not white.

SHIRLEY ADLER

We moved out in April of 1970. (*she pauses*)

   You know, you sit here and think, "Those were probably some of the best years of my life."

JEROME ADLER

No question about it. Wouldn't trade 'em.

KEITH ROBERTS

Besides everybody leavin', you had the Vietnam War, and 1970 was the last year for student deferments. I don't know why, but I got it into my head that I wanted to go to Dartmouth, so that was the only school I applied to. I got in, but it was $2,400 a year. When I told my mother what it was gonna cost she looked at me like, "I can't do it." So, knowin' that I wasn't gonna go to Dartmouth, I bought into the idea that I shouldn't go to college at all, that I should go into the service and learn a trade because that's what a lot of my black friends were doin', and that way I would just be regular. Then my draft number came up 11. So, I told my mother I was goin' into the service, and boy, she just cried and cried.

   Jane really fought me about this too, because she thought I was better than the service. And then my mother called my brother and two cousins who *were* all in the service, and they came over and beat the hell out of me. (*laughs*) So that fall, when

Jane left for Boston, I gave in and enrolled at the University of Illinois Circle Campus in Chicago.

Talk about dreams dyin'. After the experience at Bowen where blacks and whites—especially Jews—really got along and understood each other, Circle was the most racist place I'd ever been. Not only was it understood that whites and blacks didn't talk to each other, but you'd walk into the cafeteria and there would be whites over here, West Side blacks over there, South Side blacks on the other side, and then the East Side over here. Man, it was horrible. See, that's how the rest of the city had actually segregated itself. But at Bowen we didn't know about this. And I'd talk to Jane in Boston and she was experiencin' a similar thing. So we felt like we had come out of this Age of Aquarius sort of thing, and it was like, "Welcome to the world." I'm tellin' you, goin' to Circle showed me how unique Bowen's racial mix really was.

10

Endgame, 1971–1972

LAWRENCE

By the fall of 1970, the beginning of my junior year at Bowen, I had a small group of friends left in the neighborhood, most of whom were seniors, and we were spending more and more time on weekends driving out to the suburbs looking for something to do. At this point I was growing steadily disinterested in studying, but I was able to maintain a B average because the overall scholastic level of the school was falling; and I was now on Bowen's varsity basketball team, although my passion for the game was gradually being replaced by an equally passionate desire to become a musician. The alienated melancholy of the late-sixties singer-songwriters had become my personal theme music.

MARILYN KIER

(*irritated*) Those of us who stayed and were involved with the JCC felt very resentful of the people who were leaving. We felt,

"If you're going to move out to Flossmoor, then go build your own center! Don't think that you can just leave here and take this one with you"—which is what some people wanted to do.

But the truth was, you couldn't support a Jewish center that had a $250,000 budget with only fifty Jewish families. We tried, but we couldn't do it. So we arranged this meeting with some prominent people from the black community to talk about how we could transfer the J to them for a dollar, and that way the black community could have what we had. But at that meeting one of our board members all of a sudden exploded and said to the black people there, "It's all your fault. You're pushing us out. You're pushing us out." It was ugly. It was *awful*. There's this dead silence. . . . All I could say to these people was, "He doesn't represent everybody."

Ultimately the black community couldn't get themselves together, and the building was sold to the Board of Education. I'm sure the Jewish families that were left felt we were abandoning them. But the J was the last institution in the area to close. By the fall of '71 it was gone.

DARNELL WILSON

I came back to the neighborhood in 1971 after a coupla semesters of college, and I was workin' again at Mr. D's on 87th Street; and pretty soon I realized, "Oh, they don't live here no more. Fine." See, me and my friends, we was tryin' to begin our adult lives and get settled in, so it didn't bother us, because the people who had moved into the neighborhood was a lotta middle- and upper-middle-class blacks, and some of the Jewish-owned businesses that was leavin' was bein' replaced by black-owned ones.

LAWRENCE

At the start of my senior year at Bowen, in the fall of '71, I made a point of knowing how many absences could cause a mandatory failure for a student in the Chicago Public School system. The answer was forty days absent. My senior year I missed thirty-nine. I did not want to be there. The last of my neighborhood friends had gone off to college that fall; school itself had a very loose grip on my attention; and, probably more to the point, I felt like I didn't fit in, and in my alienated frame of mind I didn't want to fit in. All the institutions that had been the centers of my world—the Youth Center, the synagogue, the local AZA chapters, and the JCC—had closed within the preceding eighteen months; and at Bowen I removed myself from participation in any extracurricular activity. My status that year was that of a former basketball player, a former student council member, a former mixed-chorus member, a former Spanish Club member—in fact, I was a former student in all but name.

With virtually all the Jews gone, tension was building at Bowen between rival black and Latino factions that were starting to vie for turf dominance. I always had in-school friendships with blacks and Latinos, and I never personally felt in any danger—but I knew what bathrooms and hallways to stay out of, and what streets not to go down. Also, my long hair seemed to brand me as part of a small, fringe, hippy faction in the school, so the tough guys mistakenly assumed I was either taking or selling drugs—two activities that they respected—and they left me alone. The only time I was ever physically attacked at Bowen was by two cops who patrolled the area around the school and hated the way I looked.

RICHARD GOLD

I was unprepared for how much Skokie was a completely different world from the South Side. The first day I was at Niles East High School I went to a pep rally, and there were 2,200 white faces there, and they all looked alike. I felt completely isolated.

Also, geographically I expected Skokie to be an extension of the city. But the kids I was meeting there couldn't believe I knew my way around the streets of Chicago. They were fascinated that I personally knew blacks or Mexicans, or that I liked to go downtown. For these people, getting on the train or the bus and coming downtown was an idea as farfetched as a lunar expedition. I was astounded that they could live twelve miles from the center of the city and have no clue what the city was.

LAWRENCE

I was robbed twice at gunpoint during the fall of my senior year. The first time I was working on 87th Street at Mr. D's with Darnell Wilson, and I was so unprepared for a robbery that when I saw two guys approach the counter and take guns out of their jackets, my first thought was that those were toy guns and that this was a prank. It was only when one of them cocked his gun at my temple that I realized this was the real thing.

The second time was on the North Side of Chicago when two white guys trapped a friend and me in the vestibule of an apartment building. They were very high, waving guns, blocking the exit, and raving about how they had been fucked over in Vietnam, and that someone had to pay. Somehow my friend and I convinced them that we weren't the enemy, that Nixon was the enemy—and after about twenty minutes they took our money and stumbled away.

RICHARD GOLD

Living in Skokie was so different from the South Side that it actually gave me an extraordinary sense of what I had before, and what was valuable about each place. But I would never, to this day, say I was from Skokie. I went to Skokie to finish high school—that was it. It was like living in a hotel for two years. On the other hand, the South Side had been such a rich environment to begin with that once everyone was gone and that richness was depleted, you felt its absence. By far the South Side was the lonelier experience.

LAWRENCE

I started to experience terrifying anxiety attacks soon after the second robbery—extreme heart palpitations, cold sweats, inability to breathe. I didn't understand what was happening. I didn't know if these attacks were an aftereffect of the holdups or just a physical manifestation of feeling terribly lost and isolated.

My mother was especially concerned about me. We had awful arguments over the extent to which I was "floundering," to use her word. She could see that I was very unhappy. She thought it had all to do with the way the neighborhood had changed—I wasn't so sure it was that simple—and she feared that my father and she had made a mistake by not moving.

I got through the year by leaving the city as often as I could and spending as many weekends as possible with some new musician-friends of mine who were attending the University of Illinois in Champaign-Urbana; and I was counting off the days until graduation when I could move down there myself.

MARILYN KIER

What happened was, by '72 our youngest daughter was already going to the University of Chicago High School, and she had a couple of unpleasant incidents where she was harassed on the bus on the way home. Then somebody came to the door of our house, she felt threatened—whatever it was, we left, and we moved to Hyde Park, which at least is an integrated situation. But I could hardly bear to tell the nice young couple that had moved next door to us that we were going. I was ashamed. I don't think I was very nice then. I had a lot of anger at the people who ran. By the time we left, we were one of the few white families still on the block.

You know, I find myself getting aggravated even as we talk about this. (*laughs*) But I think what I found so upsetting about those years is that so many of the people who left weren't even willing to give it a try.

LAWRENCE

The years leading up to my seventeenth birthday in 1972 had of-
fered the escalation of the Vietnam War, the assassinations of
King and Bobby Kennedy, the riots in Grant Park during the
1968 Democratic Convention, Nixon's election, FBI wiretaps, the
Pentagon Papers, the murder of Black Panther Fred Hampton by
Chicago police, Kent State, and countless other frightening,
chaotic, and disillusioning events in America. The idea of trusting
established institutions of authority, such as the police, schools,
government, the presidency, the military, religion—or even community, *seemed impossible to many people my age. And my own*
personal experience reflected this general sense of chaos, for my
community had crumbled under what appeared to be the weight
of its own moral, political, and religious hypocrisy. Nothing that I
could point to in what had once been my world seemed to suggest
that the alienation and depression I was feeling wasn't completely
justified.

LOUISE DREYER

We stayed until 1972. Our youngest daughter was about to enter
high school, and I wanted her to have a public school education. I
felt she had to grow up in the real world. And I needed a congregation that I could walk to, and the ability to walk to a grocery
store where I could get the kosher foods I wanted, because the
grocery stores already were changing the kinds of foods they
were carrying, catering more to the blacks, and this was a problem, especially when it came time for the High Holidays.

Some people were saying, "How bad can your neighbors be if
they can afford these houses?" And the people who lived next
door to us were a refined, educated, well-to-do couple. But also,
some were moving in with a couple of families together. We sold
our house to—we're not sure what mafia they belonged to, because they came down to the closing—he had diamonds on every
finger and a suitcase full of cash. That's how he paid for the

house. I thought, "Oh God, who did I sell my house to?" (*almost crying*) This lovely home of mine—I had painstakingly put into it everything I wanted. It was a terrible, wretched feeling the day we walked out of there. Literally, that day, and the day I saw the last plaque come off the congregation wall, were the worst days I had ever known.

But I had no choice. I had to leave. And there weren't too many more white families on our block by the time we left. We stayed until the bitter end.

LAWRENCE

I never went to have my picture taken for my senior class yearbook, so there is no visual record of me even being at Bowen that final year, which seems to make my high school disappearing act complete. But I did attend the commencement ceremony. It was held the last week of June 1972. A few days later I boarded a train bound for Champaign-Urbana and the University of Illinois.

I was proud that my family still lived in the neighborhood, and that I had graduated from Bowen. But for me, this was the train to freedom. I had my ticket, and after a year of waiting, it was finally time to leave.

11

Aftermath, 1973–1995

LAWRENCE

My family finally sold our house on Chappel in 1975 and moved to an apartment a few miles away in the Hyde Park area of the South Side. All that was left of our old community at that point were a few white families scattered about the area. But the leaving was still painful, especially for my mother. Giving up on the neighborhood and letting go of her dream house meant, to her, that she was giving up on two of her most treasured dreams—to grow old with my father in the community they had lived in and felt part of for most of their married life, and to have our house be the home where her children would someday bring her grandchildren to visit. My mother's sense of loss over leaving hovered about our family for many years.

LOUISE DREYER
We're all displaced.

ARTHUR DREYER
Since we moved north, I've been on the board of three congregations without any emotional attachment.

LOUISE DREYER
All our old friends feel dislocated. None of us have found a congregation that we're comfortable with.

ARTHUR DREYER
We've all gone through two or three synagogues.

LOUISE DREYER
Or none at all. Every Rosh Hashanah we all say, "Why don't we start our own congregation. We'll get some prayer books and we'll pray."

ARTHUR DREYER
It's the difference between being a spectator and a participant.

JEROME ADLER
Once we came to the southern suburbs, she wouldn't even go to a sisterhood meeting.

SHIRLEY ADLER
Too many painful memories. Instead I put my energy into running a Jewish organization.

JEROME ADLER
I was the same way. Wouldn't even go on the synagogue board.

SHIRLEY ADLER
We gave our money—but, Jerry, you lost heart with rabbis.

JEROME ADLER
(*quietly*) Oh, man. When Aaron Fineman left, it hurt. And then what we went through with Schechter—man alive. . . .

In the Orthodox community where I grew up, the rabbi was the *rabbi*. Then I got to the point where I felt, "Hey, he's just a person with a job; and if you put them on a pedestal, you're making a mistake."

But the whole South Side experience left you bitter for a while. You felt, "How come we worked so hard and did so much to help the community build, and it was such a short span of life?" And the bitterness got directed at Judaism. I came away with a different feeling, you know, "What's Judaism? What does it mean?" It took me a while to get over that. So instead of getting involved with a synagogue out here, I built a youth center for the area—that was kind of nice.

But you know, after all those years of being really involved with a shul, I have this feeling now of "God forbid something should happen to me, I don't want some rabbi out here to bury me."

SHIRLEY ADLER
You don't have a rabbi that knows you.

LOUISE DREYER
There are scars—that's the word, scars. As if a wound was inflicted—and I don't think it's totally healed, because I have to say, I never found myself. The High Holidays come now, and it doesn't have the same meaning.

ARTHUR DREYER
We've lived here twenty-three years. I know a handful of people on this block.

LOUISE DREYER
I felt like I was forced from my home. And I hate to admit it, but I—I—I haven't totally let go of my prejudice yet. I'm being honest. I . . . have no great love. We'd still be there—just like we've stayed here.

RICHARD GOLD

I think of that moment—the synagogue closing and our moving—as the time when I started drifting away from Judaism. It
wasn't conscious, but watching the neighborhood change, I became aware of how hypocritical people could be in terms of the
divergence between their religious views and their everyday
lives; and that hypocrisy was an absolute turnoff to me.

It troubles me how far I've drifted away from the religion. As
emotionally connected as I was to it as a kid, there's that much of
an emotional disconnection now. And then you wake up one day
and look at your wife who isn't Jewish—and the sad thing is, I
love her dearly, and I'm as happy as I can be with her, but do I
wish that I could have married a Jewish woman? Yeah. But
I didn't. Do I wish I were more religious? Yeah—but I'm not. It's
not there anymore. And the issue for me isn't whether or not I
care that my wife isn't Jewish. What bothers me is that I wish I
cared more that she isn't. And it's not that I have a problem with
Judaism itself—again, my problem is with the hypocrisy of the
people who describe themselves as deeply religious. And the first
signs of that kind of hypocrisy, like it or not, came with the
breakup of the neighborhood.

JANE WYSOCKER

The hypocrisy, the racism—and the feeling my friends and I had
that our actions were changing the world—I think all of this is
what led me toward the kind of political and social justice work
that I do in my law practice. A lot of the work has been about trying to support community organizations on a grassroots level,
black and white. But one thing I've realized in the course of
working with various communities is that a major quest in my life
is to find a community I can feel part of, and that what I'm probably doing is trying to replace the one I had and loved when I was
a kid.

I've searched for this with political groups and with friends;

but based on what I've experienced through working with lots of different communities, I've come to believe that church-based communities are the strongest, that people in that environment seem to offer the most support for each other, and have genuine ties that bind; and that these groups actually end up doing the most effective political work. So I find myself getting involved now with a progressive synagogue in my neighborhood in Brooklyn, and its social-action program—and the thing that I think a lot of us in this group seem to have in common is the goal of nurturing community and becoming involved together.

You know, it's been twenty-five years since I left that neighborhood. When I think back on what happened, am I less angry now? (*she pauses for a moment*) No. I still think, "God damn it, that community should have stuck together." I am more understanding now of why people left—their concerns over property values and safety. But they blew it. What was there was really special. Why didn't it hold?

DANIEL MAYER

For me, the South Side until the mid-sixties was kind of an idyllic setting. It was family, and neighborhood, and Jewishness, and an innocence in America—a sheltered time. And then the neighborhood changing, along with that whole ten-year period from Vietnam to Watergate, politicized me. In a sense I took a stand away from the culture we grew up with, away from the Jewishness and the status bullshit that surrounded it. I didn't want to identify myself with people who behaved in a way I found repugnant, blatantly racist. I didn't want to be *of* them.

But as I've gotten older, I've realized that I was stereotyping—that as much as those people were leaving the neighborhood because they were stereotyping blacks, I was stereotyping middle-class Jews who might feel justified in getting their families out of there if there's going to be a riot on 87th Street. "Judge not lest ye be judged." Maybe the part of me that was afraid to go to a black neighborhood at 63rd Street was racist.

But you know, when I think about that neighborhood now, for me, it's fairy-tale land. If I want to think about when I was ten or twelve and go back to fairy-tale land, I'll take a drive around there; if not, there's no point.

LAWRENCE

I first drove back to the area to take a look around a few years after our leaving, and then it was really curiosity more than anything that brought me there. But gradually I found myself drawn back to the neighborhood whenever I visited Chicago. And with each drive back I was more and more struck by how completely unchanged the area was, how well cared for it was, and how it had become surprisingly beautiful. For me, the physical beauty of the neighborhood acted as a kind of living monument to the senselessness of the flight; and anytime I thought about what had happened, all roads of responsibility still seemed to lead back to the Jewish community's failure to live by its principles.

So even though there was a peculiar kind of comfort I found in occasionally going back, the visits also disturbed me. I think, more than anything, I hated feeling like a stranger in a place that was once so completely my home.

DARNELL WILSON

I've worked here on 87th Street, ownin' my own business and all for most of the last twenty-seven years; but last year, when I found out the old Mr. D's space was for sale, I was elated. I said to myself, "This is God's gift." So it took me all this time, but I'm back where I started, and now I own the business *and* the building.

You know, I feel I was lucky to grow up in this community. It did me a lotta good, because I got a chance at a young age to intermingle with other races, where a lotta young folks that grow up in segregated neighborhoods never get that opportunity, and then they only know about these other races from what they hear. And a lotta what people hear are myths.

It helped me adapt to things. I learned the retail trade, which I'm still in. And I learned from two Jewish guys; and a lotta the business things that they taught me, I use every day.

And I would say this community is even stronger than when it was a Jewish community. It is still a viable community, and it will remain a viable community because we're not gonna do like the Jewish community. We're gonna stay. If you stay, and if you put somethin' back, you have a community.

WILLIAM GALLOWAY

I would say for the first eighteen to twenty years here we had a beautiful time.

JEANINE GALLOWAY

It's been really a joy to me—quiet, private. . . .

WILLIAM GALLOWAY

Our neighbors have been mostly African-American professionals, and we had a lot in common in terms of wanting to maintain and really improve the neighborhood as a whole.

JEANINE GALLOWAY

And we raised our children in a similar way, pushing them to pursue activities that would help them better themselves and build self-respect and discipline. Also, most of us sent our kids to private or magnet schools where there was more parental involvement in the education—

WILLIAM GALLOWAY

—and where, unlike the public schools, race wasn't a big issue. A lot of black professionals didn't trust the powers that be at the Chicago Board of Education—and there were a number of us in this community that made our lives working for the Board of Ed. We knew that available money is not put to best use. We understood that no predominantly African-American school would get the same amount of funds and resources as a similar white school would; and that there was too much emphasis on nonclassroom activities like teachers as counselors, social workers—not just educators educating. The irony is that by sending our children to private schools, I think we helped perpetuate the notion that when blacks move into an area, the public schools in that area decline, because that's exactly what happened at Bowen by the time I left there in 1974.

JEANINE GALLOWAY

The same thing happened at Warren Elementary. It was more like the kids who couldn't get into private schools went there—and they were considered bad, more dangerous. If you went to a private school it was, "Stay away from anybody who goes to Warren, you might get beaten up." And to the Warren School kids, the one who went to private school was the "privileged black child." This is how our children and their friends were perceived. They were considered "uppity." The Warren kids called them "bourgies"—for bourgeois.

WILLIAM GALLOWAY

See, in every community problems and tensions develop, factions emerge, crime becomes an issue, you become concerned about who's moving in and out. That's why by the late seventies or early eighties the residents around here started to unify in a kind of ad hoc way—I think this was part of our response to the whites leaving. We jealously protected the neighborhood. A stranger walking around on the block would attract attention. News that someone was renting a house would be met with opposition because renters don't have the same stake in keeping up the property. But I'd say the issue that really unified us—this block in particular—was Stony Island Park.

LINDA MARTIN

We moved onto Chappel in 1972, and it wasn't long before we started noticing a kind of unity among the residents here that we hadn't seen over on Ridgeland. And what really pulled this block together—(*looking at Gerald*) with some exceptions—was problems we were having with the basketball courts over at the park. This would have been the late seventies. People were starting to use them at all hours of the night, and they were beginning to bring an element to the park that wasn't kosher.

Now, I don't want to get into a class thing, but—see, there are houses of lower value four or five blocks south of here. And what happens is—(*looking over at Gerald*) this is *my* perception— there seems to be a marked difference in values between the lower-income blacks and the upper-income blacks. But everybody uses the park. So we started to get concerned about a criminal element comin' into our area, and we had to do something about it. Bill Galloway was really our champion in these kinds of fights.

GERALD MARTIN

Galloway overreacted to a lot of things. The purpose of the park is so that people can use it.

LINDA MARTIN

Also, the city started holdin' a big summer festival there in the eighties, which did bring that element of—we would commonly say gang activity, because it was a gatherin' of folks.

GERALD MARTIN

Just because we had a lot of black folks gatherin' doesn't mean we had gangs.

LINDA MARTIN

Gerald, the police were here constantly—

GERALD MARTIN

I'm sayin' there was no reason why the police was there except for that sense that where black folks are gatherin' you have gang activity.

LINDA MARTIN

You know very well we had to come together in the eighties to hold on to the neighborhood.

GERALD MARTIN

My point is that we're bein' just like white people when we say that these or those people shouldn't use the park, or when we're talkin' about a certain "element" comin' in. A certain group of blacks thinks they're the chosen ones, and any other group that wears their hair a certain way is a bad element. Whites probably felt that about us when we were movin' in here. It's all about knowledge. If you get to know a person, that person might be okay. But once more and more people are usin' the park, someone who lives a mile away comes here and suddenly everybody's thinkin', "They in my park. We got a problem with the park."

LINDA MARTIN

By the mid-eighties people didn't even feel safe walkin' there after dinner.

GERALD MARTIN

What I'm sayin' is that everybody sits in judgment of everyone else.

LINDA MARTIN

Well, you certainly did. If there was a group of people sittin' and drinkin' and smokin' cigarettes in front of our house, you might say somethin' to them.

GERALD MARTIN

Shit—I'd only do somethin' when what was goin' on affected me and my personal movement.

LINDA MARTIN

Well, that's how Bill Galloway felt!

WILLIAM GALLOWAY

Once the city started holding that summer festival here in the mid-eighties, it was like the area had been discovered, and it hasn't been the same since. People come here from all over the South Side now, and the park is always in use—even at three or four in the morning.

JEANINE GALLOWAY

89th Street's almost like a thoroughfare now. It's noisy, and since we're right on the corner, people throw stuff on our lawn—

WILLIAM GALLOWAY

And there's increasing concern about the things you always hear about—drugs, gangs, break-ins. This isn't so much in the immediate neighborhood, but it's coming in from the surrounding areas and we're slowly being torn apart.

JEANINE GALLOWAY

And now the banks are startin' to let people move into the area who are only puttin' five hundred or a thousand dollars down for a house. This permits people to buy who are overextended. We're not sayin' they're not nice people, but it sets them up for failure, and when their house goes to pot it puts the value of the whole neighborhood in danger.

Also, this economic change is bringin' in people who are from different experiences too, who just let their kids run wild—which is what nobody on this block has ever done.

WILLIAM GALLOWAY

The thing is, we always felt from the very beginning that if you don't give something up, you never lose it. If you give up a neighborhood, or an area—

JEANINE GALLOWAY

(*passionately*) So that's why we have fought for this neighborhood—I mean, we have fought some with everybody since we've been here; we have fought so much that I'm tired of fightin'. But there are times when we've had to say, whether it was the Park District or other black people or whoever: "No. This is NOT GONNA HAPPEN here, 'cause I'm gonna fight you all the way." If we wanted the community to be a certain way, we had to stand our ground.

So I guess what I'm wonderin' is—and I'm askin' you a question now. Why didn't your community look around and say, "This is happenin' here, boy, and we're gonna have to turn this around"—because for a long time the neighborhood only got better, and I think we all would have been very good together. I mean, we could have learned a lot from each other. So what I guess I'm wonderin' is, or what I'm askin' you is—why?

ARTHUR DREYER

Jews don't stay. They just go. I've studied American Jewish history. It happens over and over. The neighborhoods are like people. They become obsolete.

JANE WYSOCKER

It's that fear of someone who isn't just like you.

ARTHUR DREYER

Jews historically don't have an attachment to the land. My folks were the first in my family to even own property.

RICHARD GOLD

They watched the Martin Luther King riots on TV, and then they looked out their window and saw black people moving in next door.

MARILYN KIER

People were afraid crime would go up.

Aftermath

LOUISE DREYER
I never had experience with blacks before.

ARTHUR DREYER
A lot of the people had come out of neighborhoods that were virtually 100 percent Jewish.

MARILYN KIER
The mind-set became, "The schools will change—I want out."

RICHARD GOLD
Property values: "I'd better leave now or else I'll have to give my house away, or they'll burn it down."

DANIEL MAYER
That generation wasn't violent or malicious, but they didn't want to live with the "schvarzes."

SHIRLEY ADLER
The blacks who were moving in didn't want us. They didn't care if we stayed. They told us it was our problem.

ARTHUR DREYER
Some had bad associations from the way other Chicago neighborhoods had changed.

MARILYN KIER
Their economic status had grown—they could afford a different life-style.

JEROME ADLER
And all the SECOs . . .

DANIEL MAYER
It was inevitable.

SHIRLEY ADLER
You wanted to go where the Jews were.

JEROME ADLER
All the Rabbi Finemans . . .

DANIEL MAYER
It was the movement of this city.

SHIRLEY ADLER
People wanted to live with their own.

JEROME ADLER
It was gonna happen.

DANIEL MAYER
Black people were on the South Side and they were going to keep
moving . . .

ARTHUR DREYER
If you had to identify one emotion, it was fear.

JANE WYSOCKER
Racism.

JEROME ADLER
I fought for integration.

SHIRLEY ADLER
I think it was fear.

RICHARD GOLD
Hypocrisy.

JEROME ADLER
I fought for the temple.

LOUISE DREYER
People had fear.

DANIEL MAYER
The riots scared the hell out of people.

JEROME ADLER
Part of it may have been fear.

RICHARD GOLD
I think it was fear, fear, fear and suspicion.

LAWRENCE
And a failure of leadership.

The few Chicago communities that managed successfully to integrate and not be destroyed by flight had a leadership with a passionate, burning commitment—both economic and moral—to the survival of the community.

I said this to Rabbi Fineman—he was the last member of the Jewish community I interviewed—and after a moment of silence, he slowly replied:

"There comes a time when every generation of fathers disappoints the sons, and the sons must learn that the fathers have clay feet."

JEANINE GALLOWAY
When you talk to other people, you begin to understand some of the influences they have had; and that really, your concerns are pretty much the *same.* But we're not around each other enough to know that, and until we get to know each other we always go in for stereotypes. It's kind of unfortunate.

WILLIAM GALLOWAY
The average person doesn't have the life experiences to know that it's the things we have in common—not the differences between us—that make us what we are.

But what happened here, it wasn't a personal thing. And understanding that is what got us through a lot of difficult times. What happened was a result of what people viewed us as representing. But it's not what I was, it's not what we were, and it's not what they might think I am today.

LAWRENCE

There is a moment at the end of my time with the Galloways when I look out their picture window and am nearly overcome with emotion. I suddenly feel a profound sense of release—a deep connection to a vanished past, and an almost uncontainable sense of happiness at again being welcome inside a home on the 8900 block of Chappel Avenue.

When I finally leave it is mid-afternoon, and instead of immediately driving away, I begin walking down the block in the direction of my old house. I feel self-conscious at first—I am trying to ignore the feeling that I don't belong here, because in fact I have this overwhelming sense that I do belong here. Everything is so familiar: the spare landscape of Stony Island Park; the houses where I used to play; the summer heat reflecting up off the sidewalk so intensely that it feels as if it could burn right through the soles of your shoes; and how distinctively quiet this neighborhood is on a hot day when no one is out and about. I know the sound of this particular quiet—it's the din of traffic coming from Jeffery Boulevard a block away, the rumble of the Illinois Central trains down at 94th Street, the occasional rev of a lawn mower starting up, distant voices that the breeze carries from the tennis courts in Stony Island Park—the same annoying silence that I wanted to escape from as a child. But now this silence makes the block feel indescribably peaceful. And nothing has changed, except the lushness of the trees and the evergreens.

I slowly walk past our old house and then keep going one block down and one block over until I am standing in front of the JCC and across the street from the synagogue, both of which are now special schools run by the Board of Education. When I ask at each place if I may look around, people are curious—it seems that no one in recent memory has made this request—but they invite me in as if I were a lost traveler returned, and seem eager not only to show me around but to show how well the buildings have been cared for. Once inside, I feel like a reverse Rip Van Winkle

who has come back after more than twenty years away and is as-
tonished not so much by how things have changed but by how
much some things have stayed remarkably the same: not only are
both places exactly as they were on the outside, but no changes
have been made on the inside. Walking into these two buildings is
almost like walking back in time. It is surprisingly moving to be
led into the gymnasium of the JCC again, find it as it had been,
and then pick up a basketball and shoot one more jump shot; or
to stand in the back of the sanctuary at the temple and watch a
choir of black children on the pulpit rehearsing their graduation
song, all the while flashing back to my Hebrew School choir re-
hearsing for our graduation in the exact same spot, with there
being no difference in the picture except for the missing ark and
torahs.

This is not what you envision when you think about going
back. You expect the places that you once knew to be completely
changed, transformed, only a vague remnant of the images in
your memory; or you expect the places to be the same but broken
down, dilapidated, victims of the crueler aspects of time.

Instead, these buildings seem to be an exaggerated micro-
cosm of the neighborhood itself. It is physically exactly as it had
been, yet it is entirely different. What existed for more than twenty
years has completely disappeared, yet it is all still here for the eye
to see.

For the next two hours I walk around the neighborhood. I feel
completely at home—at home in a way that I could never feel
anywhere else. These are the streets I walked in the time before
consciousness, before yearning or loss, before disappointment,
disillusionment, or ambiguity. These are the streets I walked be-
fore I started dreaming of walking other streets. And all of the
fears, concerns, or discomfort I once felt about traveling through
this neighborhood are gone now. For a moment it is as if I am
again part of this community, as if a place that had been lost to
me has somehow miraculously been found.

175

The South Side

KEITH ROBERTS
My wife and I still live on the South Side, but I tell people all the time that I can't stay in this city much longer. It's way too segregated for me. The racial stuff is endless, and I'm tired of it. As a captain in the Fire Department, I'm dealin' with hostile white people all the time, and they're usually lookin' for me to go "Hey, motherfucker," because that's all they expect from blacks; and when I use a kind of subtle diplomacy that I learned growin' up on the South Side, they don't know quite what to make of it. On the other end, I'm constantly encouragin' blacks in the department who want to stay isolated to assimilate. So in some ways I'm still between the two worlds, but I know the benefits of both because I've lived it. In that way—and it's a very positive way—growin' up on the South Side made me who I am today.

You know, when I think about what happened there from the perspective of bein' forty-three years old, and understandin' property values, I see why the whites thought they had to leave. But I think another big part of it was that our parents weren't brought together at a time in their lives where they could see that there really wasn't any difference between us. They weren't mixin' every day at Bowen like we were. Blacks and Jews got along there—we still do. We have a kind of kinship in persecution. We understand each other. Blacks don't have that with any other group. And if I learned anything from my experience growin' up, it's that if you allow children to be together from grade school on, they'll make long-term friendships—like Jane and me—and we'll stop havin' all these race problems.

MARILYN KIER
You know, the Jews and the Gentiles in that neighborhood acted the same. Maybe I'm more disappointed in the Jews, though. They should know better. But we are a tribe, and we build our walls no matter where we go. And then the walls get broken down

by somebody moving in. I'm telling you, if the Jews move any
farther north in this city, they'll be in Wisconsin. (*laughs*)

JANE WYSOCKER
I always get excited if I happen to meet an ex–South Sider—and I
realize it's because there's no one there anymore. Everyone's
gone. Where we grew up is no longer there.

RICHARD GOLD
I finally went back with my wife about ten years ago. We didn't
stop anywhere—we just drove around. It was weird—we were
white. But it was exactly the same. Really well kept up. Older
looking. It was beautiful. And the trees. That's what hit me on my
street—I couldn't believe the trees.

GERALD MARTIN
There are times when folks like you who used to live here want to
drive through this community where you grew up, and you want
to see that the community has made progress, that we have not
destroyed it—you want to see that. And in black communities
where people like ourselves are homeowners, these communities,
they improve. Blacks maintain them. This is a beautiful community.

LOUISE DREYER
We drove by the house on our way east a few years ago—it was
beautiful. "Look at my tree out there, it's all grown."

ARTHUR DREYER
But it's just like Tevye—you can't look back.

LOUISE DREYER
The physical structure is there, but it's no longer your home.

DARNELL WILSON
For me, this community is home. My mom and dad still live here.

My business is here. I found my wife in this community. Everything I have had, I found on 87th Street.

JEANINE GALLOWAY

I feel a sense of ownership about this community, and I express it all the time. But livin' right on the park, we're on the front lines. We're startin' to see an increase in drug dealin', more crime, people with different values movin' in. Bill's blood pressure's goin' up—the doctor's worried he's gonna have a heart attack. And he's such a watchdog, I'm afraid he'll confront the wrong person about somethin' and get himself shot. For the first time we're talkin' about movin'—maybe out to the south suburbs, I don't know. I just need some peace and quiet.

WILLIAM GALLOWAY

We've been here twenty-eight years. We're at a different stage of our lives now. When we were younger, to fight the struggle was just like breathing. After a while, it kind of wears you down.

You know, there's a saying going back to the Civil War about the government promising each black person forty acres and a mule. Well, forget the mule—just give me the forty acres. (*laughs*) I'll put my house right in the middle of it, with a moat or something around it with alligators and live wires and everything else—whatever it takes to just make sure people leave me alone. At times, that's what you feel.

SHIRLEY ADLER

I look around the southern suburbs now and I see black kids, and it's that old fear. I saw these signs before. It's a fear for my own personal world. And I think the cycle's gonna play itself out again, because they're bringing their problems with them. Gangs are coming here. I predict that in twenty years the south suburbs will be primarily black.

Aftermath

LINDA MARTIN

Sometimes I think, "What if the whites didn't move?" (*she pauses for a moment*) But our community's been here almost thirty years now—even longer than when it was a Jewish community. And I see stability in the future, maybe even another thirty years. For a lot of us this might be the last stop.

DANIEL MAYER

I've come to learn that everything is in flux all the time anyway. Any kind of security or permanence is an illusion. Nothing stays the same.

JEROME ADLER

But it seemed to me that it should have worked.

Epilogue

LAWRENCE
*Part of the legacy for the children who grew up on the South Side
is that our community vanished. No matter how idyllic one's
memory of childhood is, all roads of the story ultimately lead to
that great mass exodus, and what began the exodus was that a
few black families bought houses on the other side of Stony Island
Boulevard in 1964, the year the Civil Rights Act was passed into
law. Still another part of that legacy is that for many of us, the
South Side became a lost place.*

*I began this journey with the assumption that the Jewish posi-
tion was indefensible and that there was no justifying the community's flight—not then, not now. I had worn my anger at the
community and its leadership like a badge of honor for years,
with particular contempt for those who left early when the question of whether or not the neighborhood would change had not*

yet been answered. These people left and never looked back. They were never forced to question the assumptions that led to their leaving. For me, they are the center that would not hold that community together. "There comes a time when every generation of fathers disappoints the sons. . . ."

But I have now grown much more respectful and compassionate towards those who at least tried to stay, to those who tried to keep the community together, however brief the effort; and I see that the fears and growing sense of isolation that led to their moving were genuinely felt. I also see two groups of people, Jewish and black, each with prior assumptions about the other, neither with integration as a goal, who came together almost by accident at a moment in history when race relations in America were starting to explode.

". . . and the sons must learn that the fathers have clay feet."

When I arrive back on Chappel after my walk around the neighborhood, I stand in front of my old house for a long moment and feel deeply grateful to see it looking so well. It strikes me that if my family were here, we could take a photograph; and though the tree and the evergreens on the front lawn, along with the lines in our faces and the grey or white in our hair, would make visible the passage of time, there would be nothing in the image to suggest that we haven't been living here for the past twenty years. And it occurs to me that we don't really own these houses or these neighborhoods anyway; that we are only custodians—caretakers—and that it's our responsibility to use them, care for them, improve them, and pass them on.

I think about all the hours I spent in homes on this block over the preceding year, and I feel lucky, because, for the moment, I know I am welcome here. I am no longer a complete stranger, or a trespasser, or an interloper. I am a guest. But I also know that this journey has reached its end; that I can't keep coming back; that the neighborhood will always be a time lost, and the flight a missed opportunity; that some pain will always be associated with this place. More important, I know that I never want a visit to this neighborhood to become ordinary, to lose the sense of being something special. I never want to take for granted the good fortune of having found it again.

I walk back toward the Galloway house where I have left my car. As I approach I suddenly look up—and there is Stony Island Park. I surprise myself by muttering, "I really love it here," but, seeing it from that angle, I might as well be a child again. I stand there for a moment, not wanting to leave, not wanting to move. As long as I stand there looking at the park from that angle, the year is 1961, I am six years old, and we have just moved into my mother's dream house. For as long as that moment lasts, I am home.

Acknowledgments

I would like to thank the individuals at the National Endowment for the Arts for their generous encouragement and financial support of this project; David Oliver, Judy Gailen, Alba Biagini, and Pearl Lerner for trusting me enough to introduce me to neighbors and friends, and Alba for her generous assistance in researching the history of Chicago's Southeast Side; Joyce Bristow and Mary Kujawa for graciously welcoming me into the buildings that once were the neighborhood synagogue and neighborhood community center; Steven Goldberg, Nick Russell, Howard Pearl, Dorothy Gans, and Alvin and Charlene Saper for their enthusiastic encouragement; and Arnold Goodman for helping me understand the nature of my search.

I also wish to thank my remarkable wife and unofficial editor, Charlotte Maier, for her relentless honesty, keen judgment, high standards, and unflagging support throughout every stage of the writing of this manuscript; Ivan Dee for his constant faith in the project and for having the courage to take a chance; Philip Friedman for his perceptive reading of an early draft and his wise counsel regarding the many steps of the publishing process; Ari Roth for his thoughtful and challenging comments and his ongoing support of the theatrical version of this story; Peter Franklin of the William Morris Agency for his skill, trust, and patience; Bernie Sahlins for his careful reading, helpful remarks, and for introducing me to Ivan Dee; Art Perlman, Sheldon Patinkin, Beverly Lefkowitz, and Jeffrey Lunden for their insightful thoughts after reading an early draft; and Joel Margolis for sharing his knowledge of the history of Chicago neighborhoods.

Most important, I thank the many former and current residents of this South Side neighborhood whom I interviewed over the two-year period that I spent researching the story. All of those whose voices directly contributed to the creation of this text offered their participation with the understanding that names and biographical details would be changed, both in the interest of privacy and to allow for the creation of composite characters. So, while honoring and respecting our agreement, I emphasize that this manuscript would literally not exist without their exceptionally generous giving of time and self. To each and every one, my fellow travelers on this journey, I offer my heartfelt gratitude and deep, everlasting appreciation.

Last, I thank my brother, Alan Rosen, whose interview served as the primary source of the character Daniel, and my parents, Arnold and Judith Rosen, for all they taught me, and for staying.

L. R.

Brooklyn, New York
April 1998

A NOTE ON THE AUTHOR

Louis Rosen is a composer, lyricist, and librettist who has written a great many musical scores for theatrical productions on Broadway, off-Broadway, and at regional theatres throughout the country. He was born and grew up on the South Side of Chicago and received a Master of Fine Arts degree from New York University. His awards, commissions, and fellowships include those from the National Endowment for the Arts, the Seattle Repertory Theatre, the Gilman and Gonzalez-Falla Theatre Foundation, the Virginia Center for the Creative Arts, and ASCAP. Mr. Rosen has co-written the award-winning musical *Book of the Night* and the forthcoming *A Child's Garden*. He lives in Brooklyn, New York, with his wife and child.